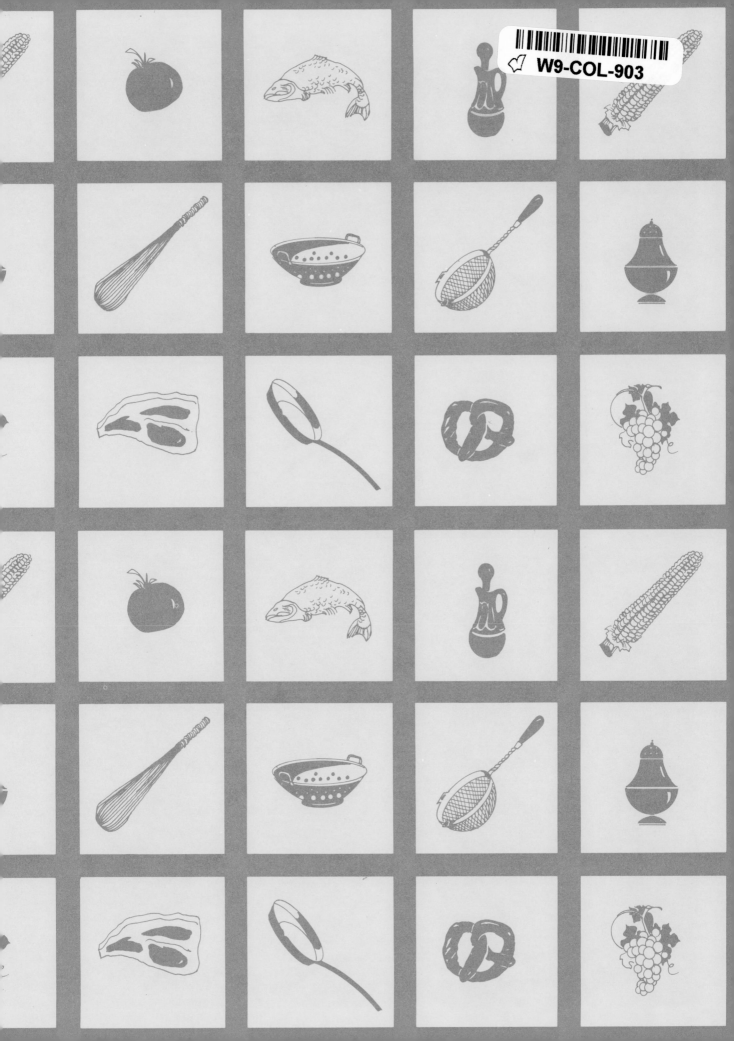

ILLUSTRATED LIBRARY OF COOKING

Cover photo: Kentucky Fried Chicken, page 12

TIME LIFE BOOKS

ILLUSTRATED LIBRARY OF COOKING

Chicken

Culinary Arts Institute®
A DIVISION OF DELAIR PUBLISHING COMPANY

Published, under agreement with Time-Life Books, by
Culinary Arts Institute
a division of
Delair Publishing Company, Inc.
420 Lexington Avenue
New York, New York 10170

The Time-Life Illustrated Library of Cooking
is a collection of tested recipes
by leading authorities in the world of cooking.
This volume contains recipes
by the experts listed below:

Michael Field, the consulting editor
for the Foods of the World series,
was one of America's top-ranking cooking experts
and a contributor to leading magazines.

James A. Beard, a renowned authority
on American cuisine, is also
an accomplished teacher and writer
of the culinary arts.

Allison Williams is the author
of *The Embassy Cookbook,*
her collection of authentic recipes
from various embassies in Washington.

ISBN: 0-8326-0806-8

Broiled Deviled Chicken

Pollo alla Diavola   *To serve 4*

8 tablespoons (1 quarter-pound stick)
  butter, melted
2 tablespoons olive oil
¼ teaspoon crushed dried red pepper
¼ cup finely chopped onions
2 tablespoons finely chopped fresh parsley,
  preferably the flat-leaf Italian type
½ teaspoon finely chopped garlic
A 2½-to-3-pound chicken, quartered
1 teaspoon salt
Lemon quarters

1. Preheat the broiler.
2. Combine the melted butter, oil and red pepper in a small bowl, and in another bowl mix together the chopped onions, parsley and garlic.
3. Add 4 teaspoons of the butter-oil mixture to the onion-parsley mixture, stir it into a paste and set it aside.
4. Wash the chicken quickly under cold running water and pat dry with paper towels.

5. Brush both sides of the chicken with half the remaining butter-oil mixture and salt it lightly.
6. Arrange the quarters skin side down on the rack of the broiler pan and broil about 4 inches from the heat.
7. After 5 minutes, baste the chicken with the remaining butter-oil mixture and broil for 5 more minutes.
8. Baste the chicken again and turn it skin side up on the rack. Then broil, basting every 5 minutes with the pan drippings, for another 10 to 15 minutes, or until the juice runs clear when a thigh is pierced with the tip of a sharp knife.
9. With a small metal spatula spread the top of each quarter with the onion-parsley paste (patting it firmly in place) and broil the chicken for another 3 or 4 minutes, or until the coating is lightly browned.
10. To serve, arrange the chicken on a heated serving platter and pour the pan drippings over it. Garnish the platter with lemon quarters.

Chicken is a worldwide favorite, often prepared in such unusual ways as this chicken marinated in lemon juice and served with egg yolks and tomatoes.

Broiled Marinated Chicken

Kababe Morgh   *To serve 4*

1 cup finely grated onion
½ cup fresh lemon juice
2 teaspoons salt
Two 2-pound chickens, each cut into 8 serv-
** ing pieces**
4 tablespoons melted butter
⅛ teaspoon ground saffron (or ⅛ teaspoon
** saffron threads pulverized with a mortar**
** and pestle or the back of a spoon)**
** dissolved in 1 tablespoon warm water**

1. In a stainless-steel, enameled or glass bowl combine the onion, lemon juice and salt, stirring until they are thoroughly blended.
2. Add the chicken and turn the pieces about with a spoon to coat them well. Marinate at room temperature for at least 2 hours or in the refrigerator for 4 hours, turning the pieces over occasionally.

3. Light a layer of coals in a charcoal broiler and let them burn until a white ash appears on the surface or preheat the stove broiler to its highest point.
4. Remove the chicken from the marinade and string the pieces tightly on 4 long skewers, pressing them together firmly. If you are broiling the chicken in an oven, suspend the skewers side by side across the length of a large roasting pan deep enough to allow about 1 inch of space under the meat.
5. Stir the melted butter and dissolved saffron into the marinade and brush the chicken evenly on all sides with 2 or 3 tablespoons of the mixture.
6. Broil about 3 inches from the heat for 10 to 15 minutes turning the skewers occasionally and basting the chicken frequently with the remaining marinade. The chicken is done if the juices that trickle out are yellow rather than pink when a thigh is pierced with the point of a small, sharp knife.

Kiev-style Fried Chicken

Poulet à la Kiev *To serve 4*

2 chicken breasts, split in half
⅛ pound sweet butter
1 clove garlic, crushed
2 teaspoons finely chopped chives or
  marjoram
Salt
Pepper
About ½ cup flour
1 egg, beaten
About ½ cup bread crumbs
Oil for deep-fat frying
Watercress

1. Skin the chicken breasts and remove the bones.
2. Place each chicken breast between 2 pieces of waxed paper, skin side down. Pound them with a wooden mallet until they are about ¼ inch thick. Remove the paper.
3. In the middle of each breast place a small piece of firm cold butter, a bit of garlic, ½ teaspoon chopped chives or marjoram, salt and pepper.
4. Roll up the meat, tuck in each end and secure with a skewer.
5. Dust lightly with flour, brush with the beaten egg and roll in bread crumbs.
6. Fry in deep, hot fat (350°) for 3 to 4 minutes until golden brown. Drain on paper towels and remove skewers.
7. Serve on a hot platter and garnished with watercress.

Eight-Pieces Chicken

Cha-pa kwai *To serve 2 to 4*

A 2½-pound frying chicken
2 tablespoons soy sauce
1 tablespoon Chinese rice wine, or pale dry
  sherry
1 teaspoon salt
1½ teaspoon sugar

1 scallion, including the green top, cut into
  2-inch pieces and split half
A ½-inch cube peeled fresh ginger root,
  crushed with a cleaver or kitchen mallet
3 cups peanut oil, or flavorless vegetable oil
½ cup flour
Salt
Freshly ground black pepper

PREPARE AHEAD: 1. On a chopping board, cut off the wings, legs and thighs of the chicken with a cleaver or large, sharp knife. Cut the body in half by cutting down through the breastbone and backbone. Then, one at a time, chop the 8 pieces of chicken across the bones into 2-inch pieces. Spread the chicken on a double thickness of paper towels and pat each piece thoroughly dry.
2. In a large bowl, combine the soy sauce, wine, salt, sugar, scallions and ginger, stirring until the salt and sugar dissolve. Add the chicken and toss the pieces about to coat them thoroughly with the mixture. Marinate at room temperature for 1 to 2 hours.
3. Have the chicken, flour and oil within easy reach.

TO COOK: 1. Pour 3 cups of oil into a 12-inch wok or deep-fryer and heat the oil until a haze forms above it or it registers 375° on a deep-frying thermometer.
2. Drain the chicken and discard the marinade. With paper towels, wipe the chicken pieces dry.
3. Dip them in the flour, then vigorously shake off all but a light dusting of the flour.
4. Drop the chicken into the hot oil and fry, in two or more batches, if necessary, turning the pieces frequently for 5 minutes, or until the pieces are golden brown on both sides.
5. Remove them from the oil with a bamboo strainer or slotted spoon and drain them on a double thickness of paper towels.
6. Season with salt and pepper to taste and serve on a heated platter.

Chicken and Sauerkraut

Podvarak   *To serve 4 to 5*

1½ pounds sauerkraut
A 3-pound frying chicken, cut up
Salt
7 tablespoons bacon fat or lard
½ cup finely chopped onions
¼ teaspoon finely chopped garlic
1 tablespoon finely chopped hot chili
  peppers
Freshly ground black pepper
½ cup chicken stock

1. Wash the sauerkraut under cold running water, then soak it in cold water 10 to 20 minutes to reduce it sourness. Squeeze it dry by the handful.
2. Wash the chicken pieces quickly under cold running water, pat them dry with paper towels and salt generously.
3. Over high heat, in a heavy 10-inch skillet, heat 4 tablespoons of the fat until a light haze forms over it.
4. Brown the chicken pieces a few at a time, starting with the skin sides down and turning them with tongs. As each browns, remove to a platter and add a fresh piece to the pan until all the chicken is done. Set aside.
5. Heat the rest of the fat in the skillet until a light haze forms over it and add the onions and garlic.
6. Cook them for 2 or 3 minutes, or until the onions are slightly translucent.
7. Add the sauerkraut, chili peppers and a few grindings of black pepper.
8. Cook uncovered for 10 minutes over medium heat.
9. Using the tongs, lay the chicken pieces on top of the sauerkraut and pour the stock over the chicken. Bring the liquid to a boil, then reduce the heat to low and cook, covered, for 30 minutes, or until the chicken is tender.
10. Serve the sauerkraut on a platter with the chicken, either surrounding it or as a bed for it.

Broiled Spiced Chicken

To serve 8

Two 2½-pound broilers, quartered
2 cups yoghurt
2 teaspoons salt
2 teaspoons black pepper
2 teaspoons ground cumin seed
1½ teaspoons cinnamon
1 teaspoon dried mint
1½ teaspoon ginger
3 tablespoons lemon juice
Oil

1. Wash and dry the chickens, then marinate them in a mixture of all the remaining ingredients except oil for 3 hours at room temperature. Be sure the chicken quarters are well covered with the yoghurt mixture, spreading it on with a knife if necessary.
2. Arrange the chicken on an oiled broiling pan, and broil on the lowest rack for 30 minutes on each side.

Austrian Fried Chicken

Wiener Backhendl   *To serve 4*

A 3-pound frying chicken, cut into 4, 6 or 8 serving pieces and skinned
¼ cup fresh lemon juice
1 tablespoon salt
½ cup flour
1 egg, lightly beaten
1½ cups bread crumbs
½ pound lard
Lemon wedges

1. In a glass, stainless-steel or enameled baking dish, toss the chicken with the lemon juice until all the pieces are thoroughly moistened.
2. Marinate about 1½ hours, turning the pieces occasionally.
3. Before frying, pat the pieces dry with paper towels, then salt them generously, dip them in the flour and shake off the excess. Then dip them in the egg.
4. Roll each piece of chicken in the bread crumbs to coat it thoroughly.
5. If the chicken is cut into 8 pieces, no cooking after frying is necessary. If it is cut into 4 (in the Austrian tradition) or 6 pieces, preheat the oven to 250° and set a large baking dish on the middle shelf.
6. In a heavy 12-inch skillet, heat the lard until a light haze forms over it. (The melted fat should be about ¼ inch deep and should be kept at that depth.)
7. Using tongs, add about half the chicken pieces. When these are a deep golden brown on one side, turn them with the tongs.
8. If the chicken is cut into small pieces, transfer each to paper towels to drain before serving. If the pieces are larger, put each browned piece into the baking dish in the oven. In either case replace the cooked piece with an uncooked one as you fry it.
9. Chicken cut into 6 pieces should be baked 5 to 10 minutes. One cut into 4 pieces should be baked 10 to 15 minutes.
10. Fry all the chicken in the same way, allowing more time for the dark meat than for the wings and breasts. The frying should take about ½ hour.
11. Serve the chicken garnished with lemon wedges.

In Austria, a quartered chicken is marinated for 1½ hours, then dipped in bread crumbs, fried and baked to produce a crisp outside, tender inside.

Southern Fried Chicken with Gravy

To serve 4

A 2½-pound frying chicken, cut into serving pieces
Salt
1 cup flour
1 cup lard, or ½ cup vegetable shortening combined with ½ cup lard

1. Wash the chicken pieces under cold running water and pat them thoroughly dry with paper towels.
2. Sprinkle the pieces with salt on all sides.
3. Put the cup of flour in a sturdy paper bag. Drop the chicken into the bag a few pieces at a time and shake the bag until each piece is thoroughly coated with flour.
4. Remove the chicken pieces from the bag and vigorously shake them free of all excess flour. Lay them side by side on a sheet of wax paper.
5. Preheat the oven to 200° and in the middle of the oven place a shallow baking dish.
6. Over high heat melt the lard or combined lard and shortening in a 10- or 12-inch heavy skillet. The fat should be ¼ inch deep. If it is not, add a little more.
7. When a light haze forms above it, add the chicken pieces, starting them skin side down. It is preferable to begin frying the legs and thighs first, since they will take longer to cook than the breasts and wings.
8. Cover the pan and fry the chicken over moderate heat for about 6 to 8 minutes, checking every now and then to make sure the chicken does not burn.
9. When the pieces are deep brown on one side, turn them over and cover the pan again.
10. Transfer the finished chicken to the baking dish in the oven and continue frying until all the pieces are cooked.
11. Keep the chicken warm in the oven while you make the gravy.

CREAM GRAVY
2 tablespoons flour
¾ cup chicken stock, fresh or canned
½ to ¾ cup light cream
Salt
White pepper

1. Pour off all but 2 tablespoons of fat in the frying pan. Add 2 tablespoons of flour, and stir until the fat and flour are well combined.
2. Pour in the chicken stock and ½ cup of the light cream, and cook over moderate heat, beating with a whisk until the gravy is smooth and thick. If it is too thick for your taste, stir in the remaining cream to thin it. Strain it though a fine sieve if you wish.
3. Taste for seasoning, then pour into a heated gravy boat and serve with the fried chicken arranged attractively on a heated serving platter.

Kentucky Fried Chicken

To serve 4

2 to 4 pounds lard
A 2½- to 3-pound chicken, cut into 8 serving pieces
2 teaspoons salt
Freshly ground black pepper
1 egg, lightly beaten and combined with ½ cup milk
1 cup flour

1. Preheat the oven to its lowest setting.
2. Line a large shallow baking dish with paper towels and place it in the center of the oven.
3. Melt 2 pounds of the lard over high heat in a deep fryer or large heavy saucepan. When melted, the fat should be 1½ to 2 inches deep; add more lard if necessary. Heat the lard to a temperature of 375° on a deep-frying thermometer, or until it is very hot but not smoking.
4. Pat the pieces of chicken completely dry with paper towels and season them on all sides with the salt and a few grindings of pepper.
5. Immerse the chicken pieces one at a time in the egg-and-milk mixture, then dip them in the flour and turn to coat them lightly but evenly.
6. Fry the chicken thighs and drumsticks, starting them skin side down and turning them frequently with tongs, for about 12 minutes, or until they color richly and evenly. As they brown, transfer them to the paper-lined dish and keep them warm in the oven.
7. Fry the wings and breast, separately if necessary to avoid overcrowding the pan. The white meat will be fully cooked in 7 or 8 minutes.
8. When all the pieces are fried, mound the chicken attractively on a heated platter and serve at once.

Chicken in Lemon Sauce

Poulet Sauté Citron *To serve 6 to 8*

Two 3½-pound frying chickens, disjointed
2 teaspoons salt
½ teaspoon pepper
2 tablespoons olive oil
6 tablespoons butter
¼ cup dry white wine
3 shallots, chopped
1 tablespoon chopped parsley
2 tablespoons lemon juice
Lemon wedges

1. Wash and dry the chicken pieces; season with the salt and pepper.
2. Heat the oil and 3 tablespoons of the butter in a large skillet.
3. Place the chicken pieces in it in a single layer and brown on all sides.
4. Cover and cook over low heat until tender, about 45 minutes.
5. Arrange the chicken on a hot serving platter and keep warm.
6. To the pan juices, add the wine, shallots and parsley. Bring to a boil, scraping the browned particles in the skillet into the liquid.
7. Remove from the heat and stir in the remaining butter. When it has melted, add the lemon juice.
8. Pour the liquid over the chicken and garnish with the lemon wedges.

Chicken Breasts with Prosciutto and Cheese

Petti di Pollo alla Bolognese   *To serve 4*

2 whole chicken breasts, about 1 pound each, skinned, halved and boned
Salt
Freshly ground black pepper
Flour
3 tablespoons butter
2 tablespoons oil
8 thin 2-by-4-inch slices prosciutto
8 thin 2-by-4-inch slices imported Fontina or Bel Paese cheese
4 teaspoons freshly grated imported Parmesan cheese
2 tablespoons chicken stock, fresh or canned

1. Preheat oven to 350°.
2. With a very sharp knife, carefully slice each chicken breast horizontally to make 8 thin slices. Lay them an inch or so apart on a long strip of wax paper and cover them with another strip of wax paper.
3. Pound the chicken slices lightly with the flat of a cleaver or the bottom of a heavy bottle to flatten them somewhat. Strip off the paper.
4. Season the slices with salt and a few grindings of pepper, then dip them in flour and shake off the excess.
5. In a heavy 10- to 12-inch skillet, melt the butter with the oil over moderate heat.
6. Brown the chicken to a light golden color in the hot fat, 3 or 4 slices at a time. Do not overcook them.
7. Transfer the chicken breasts to a shallow buttered baking-and-serving dish large enough to hold them comfortably.
8. Place a slice of prosciutto and then a slice of cheese on each one. Sprinkle them with grated cheese and dribble the chicken stock over them.
9. Bake uncovered in the oven for about 10 minutes, or until the cheese is melted and lightly browned. Serve at once.

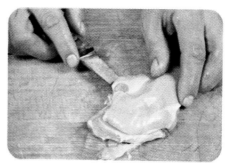

Slice the filleted breasts as indicated in the picture above.

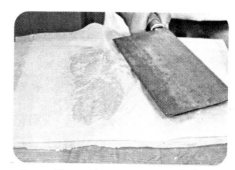

Cover fillets with wax paper; pound them thin with the flat of a cleaver.

After the fillets have been browned, cover them with prosciutto and cheese.

Braised Chicken with Kumquats

Tarnegolet Bemizt Hadarim   *To serve 4*

**A 2½- to 3-pound chicken, cut into 6 to 8
  serving pieces**
Salt
1 cup fresh orange juice
2 tablespoons fresh lemon juice
¼ cup honey
**2 tablespoons, drained, rinsed, seeded and
  finely chopped canned or bottled hot
  chili peppers**
10 candied kumquats
Lemon or orange slices

1. Preheat the oven to 375°.
2. Wash the chicken pieces quickly under cold running water, pat them completely dry with paper towels, sprinkle liberally with salt, and arrange them side by side in a baking dish large enough to hold them in one layer.
3. Mix the orange juice, lemon juice and honey together and pour it over the chicken, turning the pieces about in the mixture until they are well moistened.
4. Rearrange the chicken pieces skin side down in the baking dish and scatter the chopped peppers over them.
5. Bake uncovered and undisturbed in the middle of the oven for 15 minutes.
6. Turn the pieces over, add the kumquats and baste thoroughly with the pan liquid.
7. Basting occasionally, bake the chicken 30 minutes longer, or until the leg or thigh shows no resistance when pierced with a fork.
8. To serve, arrange the chicken and kumquats attractively on a heated platter, pour the pan juices over them and garnish with lemon or orange slices.

Chicken is given added zest in the Middle East by being baked with lemon and orange juice, hot chilies and whole kumquats, a sweet, tangy citrus fruit.

Fried Chicken Breasts with Hoisin Sauce

Chiang-pao-chi-ting   To serve 4

**2 whole chicken breasts, about ¾ pound
  each
1 tablespoon cornstarch
1 tablespoon Chinese rice wine, or pale dry
  sherry
1 tablespoon soy sauce
¼ cup peanut oil, or flavorless vegetable
  oil
1 medium green pepper, deribbed, seeded
  and cut into ½-inch squares
6 water chestnuts, cut into ¼-inch cubes
¼ pound fresh mushrooms, cut into
  ¼-inch cubes
½ teaspoon salt
2 tablespoons *hoisin* sauce
¼ cup roasted cashews or almonds**

PREPARE AHEAD: 1. One at a time, bone, skin and slice the chicken breasts in the following fashion: Lay the whole chicken breast on its side on a chopping board. Holding the breast firmly in place with your hand, cut it with a cleaver or sharp knife lengthwise through the skin, along the curved breastbone.
2. Carefully cut all the meat from the bones on one side of the breastbone.
3. Then grasp the meat in one hand and pull it off the bones and away from the skin – using the cleaver to free the meat if necessary.
4. Turn the breast over and repeat on the other side.
5. Remove each tube-shaped fillet from the boned breast meat and pull out and discard the white membranes.
6. Lay the breast meat and fillets flat and cut them lengthwise into ½-inch strips, then cut the strips crosswise to make ½-inch squares.
7. Place the chicken squares in a large bowl and sprinkle them with cornstarch, then toss them about with a spoon to coat them lightly and evenly. Pour in the wine and soy sauce, and toss the chicken again to coat the squares.
8. Place the above ingredients, and the oil, green pepper, water chestnuts, mushrooms, salt, *hoisin* sauce and cashews or almonds within easy reach.

TO COOK: 1. Set a 12-inch wok or 10-inch skillet over high heat for about 30 seconds. Pour in a tablespoon of the oil, swirl it about in the pan and heat for another 30 seconds, turning the heat down to moderate if the oil begins to smoke.
2. Immediately add the green peppers, water chestnuts, mushrooms and salt, and stir-fry briskly for 2 to 3 minutes.
3. Scoop out the vegetables with a slotted spoon and set them aside on a plate.
4. Pour the remaining 3 tablespoons of oil into the pan, heat almost to the smoking point and drop in the marinated chicken. Stir-fry over high heat for 2 to 3 minutes until the chicken turns white and firm.
5. Then add the *hoisin* sauce, stir well with the chicken, add the reserved vegetables and cook for 1 minute longer.
6. Now drop in the cashews or almonds and stir to heat them through.
7. Transfer the entire contents of the pan to a heated platter and serve at once.

Fried Chicken with Peppers

Sung-tzu-chi-ssu   To serve 4 to 6

**2 whole chicken breasts about ¾ pound
  each
½ cup pine nuts (pignolia nuts)
2 teaspoons cornstarch
1 egg white
1½ teaspoons salt
1 tablespoon Chinese rice wine, or pale dry
  sherry
½ teaspoon sugar
8-12 lettuce leaves (Boston, bibb or
  iceberg)**

4 tablespoons peanut oil, or flavorless vegetable oil
1 teaspoon finely shredded, peeled fresh ginger root
3 small, fresh, hot chili peppers, finely shredded
1 teaspoon cornstarch dissolved in 1 tablespoon cold chicken stock, fresh or canned, or cold water

PREPARE AHEAD: 1. One at a time, bone, skin and shred the chicken breasts in the following fashion: Lay the whole chicken breast on its side on a chopping board. Holding the breast firmly in place with your hand, cut it lengthwise through the skin along the curved breastbone with a cleaver or sharp knife.

2. Carefully free the meat from the bones with the cleaver.

3. Then grasp the meat in one hand, and pull it off the bones and away from the skin – using the cleaver to free the meat if necessary.

4. Turn the breast over and repeat on the other side.

5. Remove each tube-shaped fillet from the boned breast meat, and pull out and discard the white tendon in each fillet.

6. Lay the breast meat and fillets flat, and cut them horizontally into paper-thin slices. Now cut the slices into shreds about ⅛ inch wide and 1½ to 2 inches long.

7. Preheat the oven to 350°.

8. Spread the pine nuts evenly on a jelly-roll pan or baking sheet and bake them in the center of the oven for about 5 minutes, or until they are lightly speckled with brown. Be careful not to let them burn. Reserve them in a bowl.

9. Place the 2 teaspoons of cornstarch-stock mixture in a small bowl, add the chicken shreds and toss them about until they are lightly coated.

10. Add the egg white, salt, wine and sugar, and stir them with the chicken until they are thoroughly mixed together.

11. Separate the lettuce leaves, wash them under cold running water and pat them dry with paper towels. Arrange them on a serving platter and refrigerate.

12. Have the above ingredients, and the ginger, chili peppers and cornstarch mixture within easy reach.

TO COOK: 1. Set a 12-inch wok or 10-inch skillet over high heat for 30 seconds.

2. Pour in 1 tablespoon of the oil, swirl it about in the pan and heat for another 30 seconds, turning the heat down to moderate if the oil begins to smoke.

3. Add the chili peppers, stir-fry for a minute, then scoop them out with a slotted spoon and set them aside in a small dish.

4. Pour the remaining 3 tablespoons of the oil into the pan, heat for 30 seconds and add the ginger.

5. Stir for a few seconds and drop in the chicken mixture. Stir-fry over moderate heat for 1 or 2 minutes, or until the chicken turns firm and white.

6. Stir in the chili peppers and cook only long enough – about 10 seconds – to heat the peppers through.

7. Give the cornstarch mixture a quick stir to recombine it and pour it in the pan.

8. Cook for a few seconds, stirring constantly, until all the ingredients are coated with a light, clear glaze.

9. Immediately transfer the entire contents of the pan to a heated platter, and serve at once with the pine nuts sprinkled on top as a garnish and the lettuce leaves arranged attractively on another plate as wrappers.

10. To eat, each guest picks up a lettuce leaf in one hand or lays it flat on a plate. About 2 tablespoonfuls of the chicken mixture are then placed in the center of the leaf and the leaf is folded in half, enclosing the chicken within it. The lettuce is rolled into a loose cylinder that can be held in the fingers and eaten.

Chicken with Peppers

Pollo a la Chilindrón   *To serve 4*

A 2½- to 3-pound chicken, cut into 6 to 8
  serving pieces
Salt
Freshly ground black pepper
¼ cup olive oil
2 large onions, cut lengthwise in half, then
  into ¼-inch-wide strips
1 teaspoon finely chopped garlic
3 small sweet red or green peppers, seeded,
  deribbed, and cut lengthwise into ¼-inch
  wide strips
½ cup finely chopped *serrano* ham, or
  substitute other lean smoked ham
6 medium-sized tomatoes, peeled, seeded
  and finely chopped
6 pitted black olives, cut in half
6 pitted green olives, cut in half

1. Wash the chicken pieces quickly under cold running water, pat them dry with paper towels and sprinkle them liberally with salt and a few grindings of pepper.
2. In a heavy 10- to 12-inch skillet, heat the oil over moderate heat until a light haze forms above it.
3. Brown the chicken a few pieces at a time, starting them skin side down and turning them with tongs. Regulate the heat so that the chicken colors quickly and evenly without burning.
4. As the pieces become a rich brown, transfer them to a plate.
5. Add the onions, garlic, peppers and ham to the fat remaining in the skillet.
6. Stirring frequently, cook for 8 to 10 minutes over moderate heat until the vegetables are soft but not brown.
7. Add the tomatoes, raise the heat and cook briskly until most of the liquid in the pan evaporates and the mixture is thick enough to hold its shape lightly in a spoon.
8. Return the chicken to the skillet, turning the pieces about with a spoon to coat them evenly with the sauce.
9. Then cover tightly and simmer over low heat for 25 to 30 minutes, or until the chicken is tender but not falling apart.
10. Stir in the olives and taste for seasoning.
11. Transfer the entire contents of the skillet to a heated serving bowl or deep platter and serve at once.

Bright with the taste and smells of Spain, this chicken is combined with olive oil, peppers, onions, garlic, black and green olives, ham and tomatoes.

Chinese Fried Chicken with Bean Sprouts

Yin-ya-chi-ssu   *To serve 4 to 6*

2 whole chicken breasts, about ¾ pounds
  each
2 tablespoons cornstarch
1 egg white, lightly beaten
2 teaspoons salt
2 teaspoons Chinese rice wine, or pale dry
  sherry
2 cups fresh bean sprouts (canned variety
  will not do, but you may substitute 2
  cups finely shredded celery)
¼ cup peanut oil, or flavorless vegetable
  oil

PREPARE AHEAD: 1. One at a time, bone, skin and slice the chicken breasts in the following fashion: Lay the whole chicken breast on its side on a chopping board. Holding the breast firmly in place with your hand, cut it with a cleaver or sharp knife lengthwise through the skin, along the curved breastbone.
2. Carefully cut all the meat from the bones on one side of the breastbone.
3. Then grasp the meat in one hand and pull it off the bones and away from the skin – using the cleaver to free the meat if necessary.
4. Turn the breast over and repeat on the other side.
5. Remove each tube-shaped fillet from the boned breast meat, and pull out and discard the white membranes.
6. Lay the breast meat and fillets flat and cut them horizontally into paper-thin slices. Then cut the slices into shreds 1½ to 2 inches long and ⅛ inch wide.
7. Place the chicken shreds in a large bowl, sprinkle them with cornstarch and toss to coat lightly. Then add the lightly beaten egg white, 1½ teaspoons of the salt and the wine, and, with a large spoon, mix all the ingredients together gently but thoroughly.
8. Rinse the fresh bean sprouts in a pot of cold water and discard any husks that float

to the surface. Drain the sprouts and pat them dry with paper towels.
9. Have the chicken mixture, bean sprouts and oil within easy reach.

TO COOK: 1. Set a 12-inch wok or 10-inch skillet over high heat for about 30 seconds.
2. Pour in 1 tablespoon of oil, swirl it about in the pan and heat for another 30 seconds, turning the heat down to moderate if the oil begins to smoke.
3. Immediately add the bean sprouts and remaining ½ teaspoon salt, and stir-fry for about a minute.
4. Remove them with a bamboo strainer or slotted spoon to a bowl and set aside.
5. Pour the remaining 3 tablespoons of oil into the pan, heat for a few seconds and add the chicken mixture. Stir-fry over high heat for about 1 minute, or until the chicken turns white.
6. Return the bean sprouts to the pan and stir-fry together with the chicken for another minute.
7. Transfer the entire contents of the pan to a heated platter and serve at once.

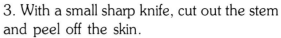

Braised Chicken with Tomatoes and Peppers

Pollo con Peperoni   *To serve 4*

2 green peppers
4 medium firm ripe tomatoes
A 2½- to 3-pound chicken, cut up
Salt
Freshly ground black pepper
¼ cup olive oil
¼ cup finely chopped onions
½ teaspoon finely chopped garlic

1. Skin the peppers by spearing them one at a time on a long kitchen fork and turning them over a gas flame, or by placing them under the broiler 3 inches from the heat, turning them until they blister and lightly blacken. In either case, use a small sharp knife to peel off the loose skin; quarter and seed the peppers, remove the white pith, and cut the peppers into ¼-inch strips. Set aside.
2. Scald the tomatoes in a large pot of briskly boiling water for 10 seconds, then lift them out with tongs or a slotted spoon and plunge them into cold water.

3. With a small sharp knife, cut out the stem and peel off the skin.
4. Quarter the tomatoes and cut away the pulp and seeds, leaving just the shells. Slice the shells into ¼-by-2½ inch strips and set them aside on paper towels to drain.
5. Wash the chicken quickly under cold running water and pat the pieces dry with paper towels.
6. Sprinkle each piece of chicken with salt and a few grindings of pepper.
7. In a heavy 10- to 12-inch skillet, heat the oil and brown the chicken over moderate heat, a few pieces at a time, starting them skin side down and then turning them with tongs. As each piece becomes a rich golden brown, remove it to a dish.
8. Now pour off almost all the fat from the skillet, leaving just a thin film on the bottom.
9. Add the onions and garlic and cook them over moderate heat, stirring constantly, for 3 minutes, or until they are soft and lightly browned.
10. Toss in the pepper strips and stir them with the onions for a minute or two.
11. Add the tomatoes and cook over moderate heat, stirring constantly, for 2 minutes.
12. Then return the chicken pieces to the pan and spread the vegetables over and around them.
13. Cover the pan tightly and simmer over low heat, basting every 10 minutes or so with the pan juices that the vegetables and chicken will soon give off. The chicken should be done in about 30 minutes.
14. To serve, arrange the chicken on a heated serving platter.
15. Using a slotted spoon, remove the vegetables from the skillet, let them drain, and spread them over the chicken.
16. Boil the liquid remaining in the pan over high heat for 2 or 3 minutes, stirring frequently, until it is thick and syrupy.
17. Taste for seasoning and pour it over the chicken. Serve at once.

Chicken in Chili and Tomato Sauce

Pollo en Adobo   *To serve 4*

THE SAUCE

6 dried *ancho* chilies
1 cup boiling chicken stock, fresh or canned
1 cup coarsely chopped onions
3 medium tomatoes, peeled, seeded and coarsely chopped, or substitute
  1 cup drained, canned Italian plum tomatoes
1 teaspoon finely chopped garlic
1 tablespoon white vinegar
1 teaspoon sugar
½ teaspoon ground coriander seeds
¼ teaspoon ground cinnamon
¼ teaspoon ground cloves
1½ teaspoons salt
¼ teaspoon freshly ground black pepper
4 tablespoons lard
A 3- to 3½-pound chicken, cut into 6 or 8 serving pieces

NOTE: Wear rubber gloves when handling the *ancho* chilies.

1. Under cold running water, pull the stems off the chilies, break them in half, and brush out the seeds.
2. With a small, sharp knife, cut away any large ribs.
3. Tear the chilies into small pieces, pour 1 cup of boiling stock over them and let them soak for 30 minutes.
4. Pour the chilies and the stock into the jar of a blender and purée at high speed for about 15 seconds.
5. Add the onions, tomatoes, garlic, vinegar, sugar, coriander, cinnamon, cloves, salt and black pepper, and blend for 30 seconds, or until the mixture is reduced to a thick purée. (To make the sauce by hand, purée the chilies, onions, tomatoes and garlic – a cup or so at a time – in a food mill set over a bowl. Then stir in the vinegar, sugar, coriander, cinnamon, cloves, salt and black pepper.)
6. In a heavy 8-inch skillet, heat 1 tablespoon of the lard over moderate heat.
7. Add the purée and cook, uncovered, stirring occasionally, for 5 minutes.
8. Remove from the heat; cover the skillet to keep the sauce warm.
9. Preheat the oven to 350°.
10. Wash the chicken pieces quickly under cold running water and pat them dry with paper towels (they will not brown well if they are damp).
11. In a heavy 10- to 12-inch skillet melt the remaining 3 tablespoons of lard over moderate heat until a light haze forms above it.
12. Brown the chicken a few pieces at a time, starting them skin side down and turning them with tongs. As the pieces turn a rich golden brown, place them in a 3-quart heat-proof casserole.
13. Pour the chili sauce into the casserole and turn the chicken about in it until the pieces are thoroughly coated with the sauce.
14. Cover the casserole tightly and bake, undisturbed, in the middle of the oven for 45 minutes.
15. Then remove the cover and bake 15 minutes longer, basting the chicken every now and then with its sauce.
16. Serve directly from the casserole or arrange the chicken attractively on a serving platter and pour the sauce over it.

Sautéed Chicken with Calvados

Poulet Sauté Vallée d'Auge　　　　　*To serve 4*

A 2½- to 3-pound frying chicken, cut up
6 tablespoons butter
2 tablespoons vegetable oil
⅓ cup Calvados or applejack
½ cup chicken stock, fresh or canned
2 tablespoons finely chopped shallots or
　scallions
¼ cup finely chopped celery
1 cup peeled, cored and coarsely chopped
　tart apples
½ teaspoon dried thyme, crumbled
2 egg yolks
½ cup heavy cream
Salt
White pepper
Watercress or parsley sprigs

1. Following the directions in the recipe for sautéed chicken with artichoke hearts (page 24), brown the chicken in 4 tablespoons of the butter and the oil in a heavy 8- to 10-inch skillet or sauté pan.

2. Pour off all but a thin film of fat, return the browned chicken to the skillet and season it with salt and pepper.

3. The next step is to flame the chicken – off the heat – with the Calvados or with apple-jack. Experts pour the Calvados over the chicken and set it alight. A more reliable technique is to warm the Calvados first in a small saucepan over low heat, ignite it with a match and pour it flaming over the chicken a little at a time, shaking the skillet gently back and forth until the flame dies.

4. Then pour in the stock and, with a wooden spoon, scrape in any browned bits clinging to the skillet. Set aside.

5. In a separate small saucepan or skillet, melt the remaining 2 tablespoons of butter over moderate heat and in it cook the shallots, celery, apples and thyme, stirring occasionally with a wooden spoon, for 10 minutes, or until the mixture is soft but not brown.

6. Spread them over the chicken, return it to high heat and bring the stock to a boil.

7. Tightly cover the skillet, reduce the heat and simmer the chicken, basting it with pan juices every 7 or 8 minutes.

8. After about 30 minutes, or when the chicken is tender, remove it from the skillet and arrange the pieces attractively on a large, heated ovenproof platter.

9. Cover the chicken loosely with foil and keep it warm in a 250° oven while you make the sauce.

10. Strain the contents of the skillet through a fine sieve set over a small saucepan, press-ing down hard on the vegetables and the ap-ples with the back of a spoon to squeeze out all their juices.

11. Let the sauce settle a minute, them skim off as much of the surface fat as possible.

12. Boil the sauce over high heat, stirring oc-casionally, for 2 or 3 minutes, or until it is reduced to about ½ cup.

13. With a wire whisk, blend the egg yolks and cream in a bowl and gradually beat in all of the hot sauce, 1 tablespoon at a time.

14. Pour back into the saucepan and cook over moderately low heat for 2 or 3 minutes, stirring constantly, until the sauce thickens to a heavy cream. Do not allow it to boil or it will curdle; if it seems to be getting too hot, lift the pan off the heat for a few seconds to cool it, stirring all the while.

15. Taste and correct the seasoning with salt and white pepper.

16. To serve, mask each piece of chicken with the sauce, and decorate the platter with bouquets of watercress or parsley sprigs.

Sautéed Chicken with Artichoke Hearts

Poulet Sauté à la Bordelaise   *To serve 4*

A 2½- to 3-pound frying chicken, cut up
6 tablespoons butter
2 tablespoons vegetable oil
16 to 24 large whole peeled shallots, or 16
  one-inch peeled white onions
Salt
Freshly ground black pepper
2 bay leaves
1 teaspoon lemon juice
1 nine-ounce package frozen artichoke
  hearts, defrosted and drained
½ cup chicken stock, fresh or canned

1. Wash the chicken quickly under cold running water and dry the pieces thoroughly with paper towels; if they are damp, they won't brown well.

2. In a heavy 10- to 12-inch enameled or stainless-steel skillet or sauté pan, melt 4 tablespoons of the butter and the 2 tablespoons of oil over moderately high heat.

3. When the foam begins to subside, brown the chicken a few pieces at a time, starting them skin side down and turning them with tongs. As the pieces become a rich golden brown, remove them to a plate.

4. When all the chicken is browned, add the shallots or onions to the skillet and cook them, shaking the pan to color them lightly and as evenly as possible.

5. Pour off all but a thin film of fat and return the chicken to the skillet.

6. Season with salt and pepper, lay the bay leaves on top and cover the pan.

7. Cook over high heat until the fat splutters. At once reduce the heat and cook the chicken slowly, using a bulb baster or spoon to baste it with pan juices every 7 or 8 minutes.

8. Meanwhile, melt the remaining 2 tablespoons of butter in an 8- to 10-inch enameled or stainless-steel skillet. When the foam subsides, stir in the lemon juice.

9. Add the artichoke hearts and toss them in the lemon butter until they glisten.

10. Season them with salt, cover the skillet, and cook over low heat for 10 to 15 minutes or until the artichoke hearts are tender.

11. After the chicken has cooked for about 30 minutes it should be done, and its juices will run yellow when a thigh is pierced with the tip of a sharp knife.

12. Remove the chicken from the skillet and arrange the pieces attractively on a large heated platter with the shallots or white onions and the artichoke hearts around them. Discard the bay leaves.

13. Pour the chicken stock into the juices remaining in the skillet and bring to a boil over high heat, scraping in any browned bits clinging to the bottom and sides of the pan.

14. Boil for 2 or 3 minutes until the sauce is reduced to about 1/3 cup. Pour it over the chicken and serve at once.

ALTERNATIVE: If you like, you may cook the artichoke hearts with the chicken. In that case, omit the 2 tablespoons of butter and the lemon juice from the recipe. Add the artichoke hearts to the chicken after it has cooked with the shallots for 15 minutes and baste them well with the pan juices. Cover and cook, basting every 7 or 8 minutes, for 15 minutes longer, or until the chicken is done and the artichoke hearts are tender.

First the chicken is browned, starting each piece skin side down.

Next shallots are swirled in the same skillet until they are golden.

Then the chicken and shallots are combined, covered and simmered.

Braised Chicken with Anchovy Sauce

Pollo alla Cacciatora *To serve 4*

A 2½- to 3-pound chicken, cut up
Salt
Freshly ground black pepper
2 tablespoons olive oil
¼ cup finely chopped onions
1 teaspoons finely chopped garlic
½ cup dry white wine
2 tablespoons wine vinegar, preferably
  white
½ cup chicken stock, fresh or canned
½ teaspoon dried oregano, crumbled
1 bay leaf
1 teaspoon slivered black olives, preferably
  Mediterranean style
3 flat anchovy fillets, rinsed in cold water,
  dried and chopped

1. Wash the chicken quickly under cold running water and pat the pieces dry with paper towels.
2. Season the pieces with salt and a few gridings of pepper.
3. In a heavy 10- to 12-inch skillet, heat the olive oil until a haze forms over it.
4. Brown the chicken a few pieces at a time, starting them skin side down and turning them with tongs. Transfer the browned pieces to a plate.
5. Now pour off almost all of the fat from the skillet, leaving just a thin film on the bottom.
6. Add the onions and garlic and cook them over moderate heat, stirring constantly, for 8 to 10 minutes, or until they are lightly colored.
7. Add the wine and vinegar and boil briskly until the liquid is reduced to about ¼ cup.
8. Then pour in the chicken stock and boil for 1 or 2 minutes, stirring constantly and scraping in any browned bits that cling to the pan.
9. Return the browned chicken to the skillet, add the oregano and bay leaf, and bring to a boil.

10. Cover the skillet reduce the heat and simmer, basting occasionally. In about 30 minutes, the chicken should be done; its juice will run clear when a thigh is pierced with the tip of a sharp knife.
11. To serve, arrange the pieces of chicken on a heated platter.
12. Discard the bay leaf and boil the stock in the skillet until it thickens slightly and has the intensity of flavor desired.
13. Stir in the black olives and anchovies and cook the sauce for a minute or so longer.
14. Pour the sauce over the chicken.

Chicken Paprika

Paprikàs Csirke *To serve 4 to 5*

A 3-pound frying chicken, cut up
Salt
2 tablespoons lard
1 cup finely chopped onions
1½ teaspoon finely chopped garlic
1½ tablespoons sweet Hungarian paprika
1 cup chicken stock, fresh or canned
2 tablespoons flour
1½ cup sour cream

1. Pat the chicken pieces dry with paper towels and salt them generously.
2. In a 10-inch skillet, heat the lard over high heat until a light haze forms over it.
3. Add as many chicken pieces, skin side down, as will fit in one layer. After 2 or 3 minutes, or when the pieces are a golden brown on the bottom side, turn them with

tongs and brown the other side.

4. Remove pieces as they brown and replace them with uncooked ones.

5. Pour off the fat, leaving only a thin film.

6. Add the onions and garlic and cook them over medium heat 8 to 10 minutes or until lightly colored.

7. Off the heat, stir in the paprika; stir until the onions are well coated. Return the skillet to the heat and add the chicken stock. Bring to a boil, stirring in the brown bits from the bottom and sides of the pan.

8. Return the chicken to the skillet. Bring the liquid to a boil again, then turn the heat to its lowest point and cover the pan tightly.

9. Simmer the chicken for 20 to 30 minutes, or until the juice from a thigh runs yellow when it is pierced with the point of a small sharp knife.

10. When the chicken is tender, remove it to a platter. Skim the surface fat from the skillet.

11. In a mixing bowl, stir the flour into the sour cream with a wire whisk, then stir the mixture into the simmering juices.

12. Simmer 6 to 8 minutes longer, stirring until the sauce is thick and smooth, then return the chicken and any juices that have collected around it to the skillet.

13. Baste with the sauce, simmer 3 or 4 minutes to heat the pieces through, and serve.

Smothered Chicken with Mushrooms

To serve 4

A 3-pound frying chicken, cut into serving pieces
Salt
Freshly ground black pepper
3 tablespoons butter
2 tablespoons vegetable oil
4 tablespoons finely chopped onion
3 tablespoons flour
1½ cups chicken stock, fresh or canned
½ pound mushrooms, thinly sliced
½ cup heavy cream

1. Preheat the oven to 350°.

2. Wash the chicken under cold running water and pat the pieces thoroughly dry with paper towels. If they are damp, they will not brown well.

3. Season them generously with salt and a few grindings of black pepper.

4. In a heavy 10- or 12-inch skillet, melt the butter and the oil over high heat.

5. When the foam subsides, brown the chicken pieces, a few at a time, starting them skin side down and turning them with tongs. Regulate the heat so that the chicken browns quickly without burning.

6. Then transfer the pieces to a shallow casserole large enough to hold the chicken comfortably in 1 layer.

7. To the fat remaining in the skillet, add the onions, and cook them, stirring occasionally, for about 5 minutes, or until they are soft and lightly colored.

8. Stir in the flour, mix well with a spoon and pour in the chicken stock.

9. Stirring constantly with a whisk, bring the stock to a boil, then turn down the heat and simmer for 2 to 3 minutes.

10. Pour the sauce over the chicken in the casserole, cover tightly and cook in the center of the oven for about 20 minutes.

11. Then scatter the sliced mushrooms around the chicken, basting them well with the pan gravy.

12. Cook, covered, for another 10 minutes until the chicken is tender but not falling apart.

13. To serve, arrange the chicken attractively on a deep serving platter. Skim the gravy of as much of the surface fat as you can and stir in the cream. Simmer a minute or two on top of the stove, stirring constantly. Taste for seasoning and pour over the chicken.

Chicken Simmered in Red Wine

Coq au Vin à la Bourguignonne   *To serve 4*

THE ONIONS
1½ pound lean salt pork, cut into lardons, 1¼-inch strips ¼ inch in diameter
1 tablespoon butter
12 to 16 peeled white onions, about 1 inch in diameter

1. Preheat the oven to 350°.
2. Blanch the pork by simmering it in water for 5 minutes; drain on paper towels and pat dry.
3. In a heavy 8- to 10-inch skillet, melt 1 tablespoon of butter over moderate heat, and in it brown the pork strips, stirring them or shaking the pan frequently, until they are crisp and golden.
4. Remove them with a slotted spoon and set aside to drain on paper towels.
5. Brown the onions in the rendered fat over moderately high heat, shaking the skillet occasionally to roll them around and color them as evenly as possible.
6. Transfer the onions to a shallow baking dish large enough to hold them in one layer, and sprinkle them with a tablespoon or 2 of pork fat.
7. Bake the onions uncovered, turning them once or twice, for 30 minutes, or until they are barely tender when pierced with the tip of a sharp knife.
8. Remove from the oven, drain off fat, and set aside.

THE MUSHROOMS
2 tablespoons butter
2 tablespoons finely chopped shallots or scallions
½ pound fresh mushrooms, whole if small, quartered or sliced if large

1. Melt the butter over moderate heat in another skillet.

2. When the foam subsides, cook the shallots, stirring constantly with a wooden spoon, for 30 seconds.
3. Add the mushrooms and cook them with the shallots, stirring and turning them frequently, for 2 or 3 minutes.
4. Add to the onions and set aside.

THE CHICKEN
A 2½- to 3-pound frying chicken, cut up
¼ cup Cognac
***Bouquet garni* made of 4 parsley sprigs and 1 bay leaf, tied together**
½ teaspoon dried thyme, crumbled
1 large garlic clove, finely chopped
2 cups red Burgundy or other dry red wine
2 tablespoons flour
½ cup beef or chicken stock, fresh or canned
2 tablespoons finely chopped fresh parsley

1. Wash the chicken in cold water and dry the pieces thoroughly.
2. Reheat the pork fat remaining in the first skillet, adding a few tablespoons of vegetable oil, if needed, to make a film of fat ⅛-inch deep.
3. Brown the chicken, a few pieces at a time.
4. Then pour off almost all of the fat from the skillet, add the Cognac and set it alight with a match; or warm the Cognac first in a small saucepan over low heat, ignite it with a match and pour it flaming over the chicken a little at a time, shaking the skillet back and forth until the flame dies.
5. Transfer the chicken to a heavy 3- to 4-quart casserole, and add the browned pork, *bouquet garni*, thyme and garlic.
6. Boil the wine briskly in a 1- to 1½-quart cups.
7. With a wooden spoon, stir the flour into the glaze remaining in the skillet in which the chicken browned, scraping in any browned bits clinging to the bottom and sides of the pan.
8. Pour the reduced wine into the skillet and

stir in the stock.

9. Over high heat, bring this sauce to a boil, stirring constantly, and cook it until thick and smooth.

10. Strain through a fine sieve over the chicken.

11. Bring the casserole to a boil over high heat, cover tightly, and place on the middle shelf of the oven.

12. After 30 minutes, gently stir in the onions and mushrooms, and moisten them well with the sauce.

13. Continue baking for another 10 to 15 minutes, or until the chicken is tender.

14. Discard the *bouquet garni.*

15. Taste and correct the seasoning of the sauce. Sprinkle with chopped parsley and serve.

Cornmeal-coated Chicken with Tomatoes

Pollo Rebozado   *To serve 4*

2 eggs
½ cup milk
2 tablespoons yellow cornmeal
1 teaspoon salt
¼ teaspoon freshly ground black pepper
A 3- to 3½-pound chicken, cut into 6 to 8 serving pieces
½ cup vegetable oil
½ cup coarsely chopped onions
6 medium tomatoes, peeled, seeded and coarsely chopped, or substitute 2 cups chopped, drained, canned Italian plum tomatoes
½ cup dry white wine
Bouquet of 3 parsley sprigs, 1 bay leaf, ½ teaspoon dried marjoram tied together in cheesecloth
1 teaspoon salt
Freshly ground black pepper

1. In a large mixing bowl, beat the eggs with a whisk or rotary beater for a minute or two only, then beat in the milk, the cornmeal, 1 teaspoon of salt and ¼ teaspoon of black pepper.

2. Pat the chicken pieces completely dry with paper towels, then one at a time dip them into the egg and cornmeal batter, and when they are lightly coated lay them side by side on a long sheet of wax paper.

3. Heat ¼ cup of the oil at high heat in a 10- to 12-inch skillet.

4. Add the chicken and regulate the heat so that the pieces brown quickly without burning. Turn the chicken frequently with tongs or a slotted spoon.

5. Transfer the chicken to paper towels to drain.

6. In a heavy 4-quart flameproof casserole, heat the remaining ¼ cup of oil over moderate heat until a light haze forms above it.

7. Add the onions and cook, stirring, for 4 or 5 minutes, or until they are soft and transparent but not brown.

8. Stir in the tomatoes, wine, bouquet, 1 teaspoon of salt and a few grindings of pepper.

9. Cook, stirring frequently, for 5 minutes.

10. Add the browned chicken to the casserole, basting the pieces well with the tomato sauce.

11. Cover, and simmer over low heat for 30 to 40 minutes, or until the chicken is tender but not falling apart.

12. Taste for seasoning and serve directly from the casserole.

Two elusively spiced dishes are the ginger-flavored pieces of chicken and broccoli with ham *(right)* and the chicken with soy sauce *(recipe page 34).*

Chicken and Ham in Green Paradise

Yu-lang-chi   *To serve 4 to 6*

A 4-pound roasting chicken, preferably freshly killed
3 slices cooked Smithfield ham, ⅛ inch thick, cut into 2-by-1-inch pieces
A 2-pound bunch broccoli
2 quarts chicken stock, fresh or canned, or 2 quarts cold water, or a combination of both
1 scallion, including the green top, cut into 2-inch pieces
4 slices peeled fresh ginger root, about 1 inch in diameter and ⅛ inch thick
¼ teaspoon salt
1 teaspoon cornstarch dissolved in 1 tablespoon cold water

PREPARE AHEAD: 1. Wash the chicken inside and out under cold running water. Dry the chicken thoroughly with paper towels.
2. Cut off the broccoli flowerettes. Peel the stalks by cutting ⅛ inch deep into the skin and stripping it as you were peeling an onion. Slice the stalks diagonally into 1-inch pieces, discarding the woody ends.
3. Have the chicken, ham, broccoli, chicken stock (or water), scallion, ginger and cornstarch mixture within easy reach.

TO COOK: In a heavy flameproof casserole or pot just large enough to hold the chicken snugly, bring the stock or water to a boil.
2. Add the scallions and ginger, and place the chicken in the pot. The liquid should cover the chicken; add more boiling stock or water if it doesn't.
3. Bring to a boil again, cover the pan, reduce the heat to low and simmer for 15 minutes.
4. Then turn off the heat and let the chicken cool in the covered pot for 2 hours. The residual heat in the pot will cook the chicken through.
5. Transfer the chicken to a chopping board. (Reserve stock.) With a cleaver or knife, cut of wings and legs, and split the chicken in half lengthwise, cutting through the breast and back bones.
6. Cut the meat from the bones, leaving the skin in place. Then cut the meat into pieces about 2 inches long, 1 inch wide and ½ inch thick.
7. Arrange the chicken and ham in alternating overlapped layers on a heated platter and cover with foil.
8. Pour 2 cups of the reserved stock into a 3-quart saucepan.
9. Bring to a boil and drop in the broccoli.
10. Return to a boil, turn off the heat, let it rest uncovered for 3 minutes, then remove the broccoli and arrange it around the chicken and ham. Or garnish the meat with only the flowerettes and serve the stems separately.
11. In a small saucepan, combine ½ cup of the stock with salt and bring to a boil.
12. Give the cornstarch mixture a stir to recombine it and add it to the stock. When the stock thickens slightly and becomes clear, pour it over the chicken and ham.
13. Serve at once.

Sautéed Chicken with Mushrooms

Poulet Sauté à la Crème   *To serve 4*

A 2½- to 3-pound frying chicken, cut up
5 tablespoons butter
2 tablespoons vegetable oil
Salt
Freshly ground black pepper
1 cup sliced fresh mushrooms
¼ cup dry white wine
¾ cup heavy cream
2 tablespoons finely chopped fresh parsley

1. Following the directions in the recipe for sautéed chicken with artichoke hearts (page 24), brown the chicken in 4 tablespoons of the butter and the oil in a heavy 8- to 10-inch skillet or sauté pan.
2. Pour off all but a thin film of fat, return the chicken to the skillet and season it.
3. Cover the skillet tightly and cook over high heat until the fat splutters. Immediately reduce the heat and cook the chicken slowly, basting it with pan juices every 7 or 8 minutes.
4. After 30 minutes, or when the chicken is tender, remove it from the skillet and arrange the pieces attractively on a heated serving platter.
5. Add the mushrooms to the skillet and toss for 2 minutes, then pour in the wine and boil over high heat, stirring in any browned bits that cling to the pan.
6. When the wine has almost cooked away, stir in the cream and cook it briskly for at least 3 or 4 minutes until it has reduced and thickened slightly.
7. Taste and correct seasoning.
8. Remove from heat and stir in the parsley, add the remaining 1 tablespoon of butter and tip the pan back and forth to blend it into the sauce.
9. Pour the sauce and mushrooms over the chicken and serve at once.

Chicken à la King

To serve 4 to 6

A 4- to 4½-pound cooked chicken or 3 cups cooked chicken or turkey
4 tablespoons butter
½ pound mushrooms, thinly sliced
½ green pepper, shredded
2 tablespoons flour
1 cup chicken stock
Salt
White pepper
2 egg yolks
½ teaspoon paprika
1 cup cream
2 to 3 tablespoons sherry
1 piece pimiento, shredded
Patty shells or thin toast (optional)

1. Cut the meat into thin strips.
2. Melt the butter. Add the sliced mushrooms and green pepper and sauté for 5 minutes.
3. Blend in the flour, off the heat.
4. Add the chicken stock and stir over the heat until the sauce comes to a boil.
5. Season with salt and a little white pepper.
6. Beat the egg yolks and paprika lightly with a fork. Slowly beat in the cream.
7. Add the egg-and-cream mixture to the sauce and cook until the sauce is thickened but do not let it boil again.
8. Add the chicken and heat thoroughly.
9. Just before serving add the sherry and pimiento. Chicken à la King can be served in patty shells or in a hot serving dish or chafing dish, garnished with triangles of thin toast.

Chicken Braised in White Wine

Pollo en Pepitoria   *To serve 4 to 6*

**A 4- to 5-pound roasting chicken, cut into
  6 to 8 serving pieces**
Salt
White pepper
1 cup flour
½ cup olive oil
2 cups finely chopped onions
1 tablespoon finely chopped parsley
1 large bay leaf
1 cup dry white wine
2 cups water
**¼ cup blanched almonds, pulverized in a
  blender or with a nut grinder or mortar
  and pestle**
2 hard-cooked egg yolks
1 tablespoon finely chopped garlic
**⅛ teaspoon ground saffron, or saffron
  threads crushed with a mortar and pestle
  or with the back of a spoon**

1. Wash the chicken pieces quickly under cold running water and pat them thoroughly dry with paper towels.

2. Sprinkle it liberally with salt and a little white pepper, dip the pieces in flour and shake them vigorously to remove the excess.

3. In a heavy 10- to 12-inch skillet, heat the olive oil over high heat until a light haze forms above it.

4. Starting them skin side down, brown 3 or 4 pieces of chicken at a time, turning them with tongs and regulating the heat so that the pieces color quickly and evenly without burning.

5. Transfer them to a heavy 4- to 6-quart casserole.

6. Pour off all but 2 tablespoons of fat from the skillet and add the onions.

7. Stirring frequently, cook them over moderate heat for about 5 minutes, or until they are soft and transparent but not brown.

8. Spread the onions over the chicken in the casserole and add the parsley and bay leaf.

9. Pour in the wine and water, and bring to a boil over high heat.

10. Reduce the heat to low, cover tightly, and simmer, undisturbed, for 20 minutes.

11. With a mortar and pestle or a wooden spoon, mash the pulverized almonds, egg yolks, garlic and saffron to a smooth paste. Thin it with ¼ cup of the casserole liquid and stir the mixture gradually into the simmering casserole.

12. Cover again, and cook for 10 minutes longer, or until the chicken is tender.

13. With tongs, transfer the pieces to a deep, heated platter and drape it loosely with foil to keep warm.

14. Bring the cooking liquid to a boil over high heat and boil briskly, uncovered, until the sauce has reduced to about half, or enough to intensify its flavor.

15. Taste for seasoning and pour it over the chicken.

16. Serve at once, accompanied if you like by hot boiled rice.

Braised Soy Sauce Chicken

Chiang-yu-chi   *To serve 4 to 6*

A 4½- to-5 pound roasting chicken, preferably freshly killed
2 cups cold water
2 cups soy sauce
¼ cup Chinese rice wine, or pale dry sherry
5 slices peeled, fresh ginger root about 1 inch in diameter and ⅛ inch thick
1 whole star anise, or 8 sections star anise
¼ cup rock candy broken into small pieces, or substitute 2 tablespoons granulated sugar
1 teaspoon sesame-seed oil

PREPARE AHEAD: 1. Wash the chicken inside and out under cold running water. Dry the chicken thoroughly with paper towels.
2. Have the water, soy sauce, wine, ginger, anise, rock candy (or sugar) and sesame-seed oil within easy reach.

TO COOK: 1. In a heavy pot just large enough to hold the chicken snugly, bring the water, soy sauce, wine, ginger and star anise to a boil, then add the chicken. The liquid should reach halfway up the side of the chicken.
2. Bring to a boil again, reduce the heat to moderate and cook covered for 20 minutes.
3. With 2 large spoons, turn the chicken over.
4. Stir the rock candy or sugar into the sauce and baste the chicken thoroughly.
5. Simmer 20 minutes longer, basting frequently.
6. Turn off the heat, cover the pot and let the chicken cool for 2 to 3 hours.
7. Transfer the chicken to a chopping board and brush it with sesame-seed oil.
8. Remove the wings and legs with a cleaver or sharp knife and split the chiken in half lengthwise by cutting through its breastbone and backbone.
9. Lay the halves skin side up on the board and chop them crosswise, bones and all, into 1-by-3-inch pieces, reconstructing the pieces in approximately their original shape in the center of a platter as you proceed.
10. Chop the wings and legs similarly, and place them, reconstructed, around the breasts.
11. Moisten the chicken with ¼ cup of the sauce in which it cooked and serve at room temperature.

NOTE: The sauce in which the chicken cooks is known in China as a master sauce and it is stored in a covered jar for use in red-cooked dishes. It will keep for 2 weeks in the refrigerator, indefinitely in the freezer.

Chicken with Black Cherries

To serve 6

3 chicken breasts, split in half
4 tablespoons butter
3 tablespoons brandy
1 small clove garlic, crushed
½ cup sliced mushrooms
3 teaspoons potato flour
½ teaspoon meat extract
1¼ cups chicken stock
¼ cup dry white wine
Salt
Pepper
1 cup pitted black cherries
¾ cup Hollandaise sauce

1. Carefully remove the skin and bones from the chicken breasts.
2. Brown slowly on both sides in 3 tablespoons of hot butter.
3. Heat the brandy in a small pan, ignite and pour over the chicken.
4. Remove the chicken from the pan.
5. Put the remaining tablespoon of butter and

the crushed garlic in the same pan and cook ½ minute. Add the sliced mushrooms and cook until they are lightly browned.

6. Blend in, off the fire, the potato flour and meat extract.

7. Add the stock and wine and stir over the fire until the mixture comes to a boil.

8. Add salt, pepper, black cherries and the chicken breasts.

9. Cover and simmer for 20 to 25 minutes, until the chicken is tender.

TO SERVE: 1. Arrange the chicken in an oven-proof dish.

2. Add the Hollandaise sauce to the sauce in the pan and spoon over the chicken.

3. Brown lightly under the broiler.

Roast Chicken with Currant-Jelly Sauce

Hønsesteg   *To serve 6 to 8*

Three 1¼-pound whole broilers
1 tablespoon salt
½ teaspoon pepper
2 bunches parsley
¼ pound butter
1 cup chicken stock
2 tablespoons flour
1 cup heavy cream
½ cup red currant jelly

1. Clean, wash and dry the chickens.

2. Rub them inside and out with the salt and pepper.

3. Cut away the stems of the parsley, then coarsely chop it. Mix the parsley with half the butter, and place one third of the mixture in the cavity of each chicken.

4. Close the opening with skewers.

5. Melt the remaining butter in a Dutch oven or heavy casserole. Brown the chickens in it on all sides.

6. Turn the chickens on their sides and add the stock.

7. Cover and roast in a 350° oven 1 hour, turning them on the other side after 30 minutes.

8. Transfer the chickens to a platter.

9. Place the pan over direct heat. Mix the flour with a little cream and stir it into the pan juices, then add all the cream and the jelly.

10. Cook, stirring steadily, to the boiling point, then cook over low heat 10 minutes longer. Taste for seasoning.

11. Cut the chickens into halves or quarters and pour the sauce over the pieces.

Chicken in Spicy Walnut Sauce

Ají de Gallina   *To serve 4*

A 3½- to 4-pound chicken, cut in quarters
5 cups cold water
2 tablespoons vegetable oil
3 teaspoons annatto seeds
8 slices fresh homemade-type white bread
2 cups milk
⅔ cup olive oil
1 cup finely chopped onions
1 teaspoon finely chopped garlic
¼ cup dried hot red chilies, seeded and ground in a blender or pulverized with a mortar and pestle
1 cup shelled walnuts, ground in a blender or pulverized with a mortar and pestle
2 teaspoon salt
¼ teaspoon freshly ground black pepper
¼ cup freshly grated Parmesan cheese
2 pounds boiling potatoes, peeled, sliced ¼ inch thick, freshly boiled and hot
3 hard-cooked eggs, each cut in 6 to 8 lengthwise wedges
12 black olives
1 or 2 fresh hot red chilies, stemmed, seeded, deribbed and cut lengthwise into strips ¼ inch wide

NOTE: Wear rubber gloves when handling the chilies.

1. In a heavy 4- to 5-quart saucepan, bring the chicken and 5 cups of cold water to a boil over high heat, and remove all scum from the surface.

2. Reduce the heat to low, cover the pan and cook the chicken for 30 minutes, or until it is tender but not falling apart.

3. Transfer the chicken to a plate, and set the stock aside for another use.

4. When the chicken is cooled enough to handle, remove the skin with a small knife or your fingers. Cut or pull the meat away from the bones. Discard the bones, and cut the chicken meat into strips ⅛ inch wide and 1 to 1½ inches long.

5. In a pan, heat the vegetable oil over moderate heat. Drop in the annatto seeds and stir for 30 seconds.

6. Reduce the heat to low, cover and simmer for 10 minutes.

7. Remove the pan from the heat, let the oil cool, strain it and discard the seeds.

8. Cut the crusts from the bread and tear the slices into small pieces. Place them in a bowl, add 1 cup of the milk and let them soak for 5 minutes.

9. Then, with a fork or your hands, mash the bread and milk to a thick paste.

10. In a heavy 12-inch skillet, heat the olive oil over moderate heat and add the onions and garlic.

11. Cook, stirring frequently, for 5 minutes, or until the onions are soft and transparent but not brown.

12. Add the pulverized or ground chilies, walnuts, salt and pepper, reduce the heat and simmer for 5 minutes.

13. Stir in the annatto oil and bread paste, then gradually add the remaining cup of milk.

14. Cook, stirring constantly, until the sauce thickens.

15. Add the chicken and cheese, and simmer, stirring occasionally, until the cheese melts and the chicken is heated through.

TO ASSEMBLE: 1. Spread the boiled potato slices side by side in a large casserole or deep platter and spoon the chicken and sauce over them.

2. Garnish the top with hard-cooked eggs, olives and chili strips.

Thin strips of chicken are the prime ingredient in this Peruvian dish garnished with sections of hard-cooked eggs, black olives and red chili strips.

A mold of chicken, cornmeal and a score of other ingredients *(recipe pages 39-41)* is trimmed with slices of orange, tomato, egg and stuffed olives.

Chicken
and Cornmeal Mold

Cuscuz de Galinha   *To serve 8*

THE CHICKEN

**A 3½- to 4-pound chicken, cut into 6 to 8
  serving pieces**
¼ cup distilled white vinegar
¼ cup fresh lemon juice
¼ cup olive oil
½ cup coarsely chopped onions
¼ teaspoon finely chopped garlic
¼ cup finely chopped fresh parsley
1 teaspoon coriander seeds
1 teaspoon dried savory
½ teaspoon finely chopped fresh mint
1 teaspoon salt
¼ teaspoon freshly ground black pepper
**1 large tomato, peeled, seeded and coarse-
  ly chopped, or substitute ½ cup chopped,
  drained, canned Italian plum tomatoes**
1 cup chicken stock, fresh or canned

THE CHICKEN: 1. Arrange the chicken in one
layer in a large shallow flameproof casserole
or skillet.
2. In a small enameled or stainless-steel
saucepan, combine the vinegar, lemon juice,
oil, onions, garlic, parsley, coriander seeds,
savory, mint, 1 teaspoon of salt and the black
pepper, and bring to a boil over high heat.
3. Pour the hot vinegar marinade over the
chicken, turning the pieces to coat them
evenly.
4. Cover the casserole tightly with aluminum
foil or plastic wrap, and marinate the chicken
for 3 hours at room temperature or 6 hours
in the refrigerator, turning the pieces occasionally to keep them well moistened on all
sides.
5. Over high heat, bring the chicken and
marinade to a boil in the casserole.

continued on page 40

6. Reduce the heat to low, and simmer, uncovered, for 10 minutes.

7. Stir in the chopped tomato and chicken stock and return to a boil.

8. Reduce the heat to low, cover the casserole, and simmer for 30 minutes, or until the chicken is tender but not falling apart.

9. Transfer the chicken to a plate, and remove the casserole from the heat.

10. As soon as the chicken is cool enough to handle, remove the skin with a small, sharp knife or your fingers.

11. Cut or pull the meat away from the bones. Discard the skin and bones, and cut the chicken meat into strips about ⅛ inch wide and 1 to 1½ inches long.

12. Strain the reserved cooking stock through a fine sieve set over a mixing bowl, then return it to the casserole.

13. Drop in the chicken strips and set the casserole aside.

THE SAUSAGE
2 tablespoons olive oil
½ pound *chorizo* or other smoked spiced
   pork sausage, sliced ⅛ inch thick

THE SAUSAGE: 1. In another skillet, heat 2 tablespoons of oil over high heat and add the sausage slices.

2. Turning the pieces constantly, brown them quickly but lightly on both sides, then remove them from the pan and spread them out on paper towels to drain.

THE CORNMEAL
4 cups white cornmeal
1 teaspoon salt
1 cup boiling water
1 cup melted butter (2 quarter-pound
   sticks)
¼ cup finely chopped fresh parsley
3 bottled Tabasco peppers, drained, rinsed
   in cold water and finely chopped

THE CORNMEAL: 1. Spread the cornmeal out in a large ungreased skillet and cook it over moderate heat, stirring it constantly with a wooden spoon for about 5 minutes. Watch carefully for any sign of burning and regulate the heat accordingly.

2. When the cornmeal is a pale golden color, stir into it 1 teaspoon of salt and slowly pour in the cup of boiling water, stirring constantly.

3. Cook over low heat, for 2 minutes, until all the moisture is absorbed.

4. Then remove the skillet from the heat and mix in the cup of melted butter and the ¼ cup of parsley.

5. Stir it little by little into the reserved casserole of chicken and stock and when they are well combined add the reserved sausage slices and the chopped Tabasco peppers.

6. Test the cornmeal mixture by rolling a spoonful of it between the palms of your hands. It should form a loose ball. If the cornmeal is too dry and crumbles, add a little chicken stock or water to the pan and mix until the cornmeal particles adhere. (Be careful not to add too much liquid; the cornmeal should be moist but not pasty.)

3 medium tomatoes, peeled and sliced
   about ⅛ inch thick
A 10-ounce can hearts of palm, drained
   and sliced into rounds ⅛ inch thick
3 hard-cooked eggs, cut crosswise into
   ⅛-inch slices
12 pimiento-stuffed olives, cut crosswise
   into ⅛-inch slices
1 cup cooked fresh green peas, or 1 cup
   thoroughly defrosted frozen peas
3 seedless oranges, peeled and cut
   crosswise into ⅛-inch slices

TO ASSEMBLE: 1. Butter or oil the inside of a 9- to 10-inch fine-holed colander and center a large slice of tomato on the bottom of it.
2. Arrange some of the sliced hearts of palm, hard-cooked eggs, tomatoes and olives in an attractive pattern around it, covering the sides as completely as possible.
3. Spoon in a third of the meat and cornmeal mixture and, with a spoon, smooth it and pack it down gently.
4. Scatter a layer of peas on top and on it arrange half the reserved hearts of palm, eggs, tomatoes and olives.
5. Spoon another third of the cornmeal mixture into the colander, pack it down, and cover with the remaining peas and other ingredients.
6. Spoon in the remaining cornmeal mixture, pack it down lightly, and cover with a large piece of foil.
7. Tuck the ends of the foil under the top rim of the colander to hold it securely in place.

TO COOK AND SERVE: 1. Place the colander in a deep pot, large enough to enclose it completely.
2. Pour enough water into the pot to come within 1½ inches of the bottom of the colander.
3. Bring the water to a boil over high heat, cover the pot tightly, and steam over low heat for 50 minutes, replenishing the water in the pot with boiling water as it boils away.
4. To unmold and serve the *cuscuz*, place a serving plate upside down over the top of the colander and, grasping both sides firmly, turn the plate and mold over. (If the handles of your colander stand up above the rim, be sure to choose a plate small enough to fit inside them. If the handles project from the sides of the colander, you can use any size serving plate you like.)
5. Rap the plate on a table and the *cuscuz* should slide out of the mold.
6. If any of the vegetable or egg garnish sticks to the colander, pry the pieces loose with the tip of a knife and replace them on the mold. If some of the garnish appears too crushed, substitute fresh slices of egg or vegetable.
7. Serve the *cuscuz* hot, accompanied by sliced oranges.

Braised Chicken in Cream Sauce

Stegt Kylling   *To serve 4*

3- to 3½-pound roasting chicken
1 tablespoon salt
8 tablespoons (1 quarter-pound stick) butter, softened
Large bunch of parsley
2 tablespoons butter
¼ cup vegetable oil
½ cup water
1 cup heavy cream

1. Wash the chicken quickly under cold running water, pat it dry with paper towels, then rub it thoroughly inside and out with salt.
2. Cream the ¼ pound of butter by using an electric mixer set at medium speed or by beating it vigorously against the side of a bowl with a wooden spoon.
3. With a pastry brush or your fingers, spread it inside the chicken.
4. Then stuff the chicken with the entire bunch of parsley, and truss it so that it will hold its shape while cooking.
5. Preheat the oven to 325°.
6. Heat the 2 tablespoons of butter and the oil over moderate heat on top of the stove in a heavy flameproof casserole or a roasting pan just large enough to hold the chicken comfortably, and put the chicken in breast side down.
7. After about 5 minutes, turn the bird on its side, holding it with two large wooden spoons or a kitchen towel to avoid breaking the skin.
8. In another 5 to 10 minutes, when this side is sufficiently browned, turn the chicken on its other side, then finally on its back for 5 minutes or so. The browning of the chicken should take about 20 minutes in all.
9. Transfer the chicken to a platter and pour off all but about 1 tablespoon of fat from the casserole.
10. In its place, add ½ cup of water and bring it to a boil, stirring vigorously to scrape up any browned bits clinging to the pan.
11. Return the chicken to the casserole, breast side up, cover it tightly and place the casserole in the oven to braise for about 1 hour. To test, lift the chicken upright out of the pan with a wooden spoon inserted in the tail opening. If the juice that runs out is yellow, the chicken is done; if still somewhat pink, braise the chicken another 5 to 10 minutes.
12. Place the chicken on a carving board and let it rest for 5 minutes or so while you make the sauce.
13. Skim and discard the fat from the pan juices, add the cream and bring to a boil, stirring rapidly and scraping up any browned bits in the bottom and sides of the pan.
14. Boil the sauce briskly for several minutes, until the cream has reduced and the sauce thickens.
15. Taste for seasoning, add more salt if needed, and pour the sauce into a heated sauceboat.
16. Untruss the chicken and remove the parsley before carving.

Roast Capon Stuffed with Herbs

To serve 8 to 12

Two 5-pound capons
1 tablespoon salt
¾ teaspoon pepper
8 cups toasted fresh bread crumbs
1½ cups minced onions
1 cup chopped parsley
1½ teaspoons thyme
1½ teaspoons sage
1 cup milk
1 pound butter, melted

1. Wash and dry the capons; then rub inside and out with salt and pepper.
2. Mix together the bread crumbs, onions, parsley, thyme, sage, milk and all but 1/4 cup of the butter.
3. Stuff the capons with the mixture and close the openings with skewers. Place them in a roasting pan, breast-side up, and then brush them with the reserved butter.
4. Place a piece of foil over the capons.
5. Roast in a 400° oven 1¾ hours, or until tender, removing the foil after the first hour of cooking.

French Roast Chicken

Poulet Rôti   *To serve 4*

A 3½- to- 4-pound roasting chicken
2 tablespoons soft butter
½ teaspoon lemon juice
Salt
Freshly ground black pepper
3 tablespoons melted butter
1 tablespoon vegetable oil
1 onion, sliced
1 carrot, cut in ½-inch chunks
1 celery stalk, cut in ½-inch chunks
1 cup chicken stock, fresh or canned

1. Preheat the oven to 450°.
2. Wash the chicken quickly under cold running water and dry it thoroughly inside and out with paper towels.
3. Cream the soft butter, beating it vigorously against the side of a small bowl with a wooden spoon until it is fluffy.
4. Beat in the lemon juice, 1/4 teaspoon salt and a few grindings of pepper.

5. Spread the seasoned butter inside the chicken.
6. Neatly truss the chicken with white kitchen string.
7. Combine the melted butter and oil and brush about half of it over the outside of the chicken.
8. Place the chicken on its side on a rack in a shallow roasting pan just large enough to hold it comfortably – about 9 by 12 inches – and place on the middle shelf of the oven.
9. After 10 minutes, turn the chicken onto its other side. Brush with butter and oil and roast for another 10 minutes.
10. Reduce the oven heat to 350°.
11. Turn the chicken on its back, brush it with butter and oil and salt it lightly.
12. Spread the vegetables in the bottom of the pan.
13. Roast the chicken, basting it every 10 minutes with butter and oil while they last, then use a bulb baster or spoon to baste it with pan juices.
14. After 60 minutes, test the chicken for doneness by lifting it with a wooden spoon inserted in the tail opening. When the juices that run out are yellow, it is done. If they are pink, cook a few minutes longer.
15. Transfer the bird to a carving board, cut off the trussing strings, and let it rest for 5 minutes or so before serving.
16. Meanwhile, make the sauce.
17. Stir the chicken stock into the roasting pan and bring to a boil over high heat, stirring and scraping in any browned bits clinging to the bottom and sides of the pan.
18. Boil briskly for 2 or 3 minutes until the sauce has the desired intensity of flavor.
19. Strain through a sieve, pressing down hard on the vegetables with the back of a spoon before discarding them.
20. Skim off as much surface fat as possible, and taste for seasoning.
21. The chicken may be carved in the kitchen or at the table. Serve the sauce separately.

Cool and tempting for a summer buffet, this dish is a blend of chicken, onions, leeks and carrots, flavored with herbs and garnished with lemon slices.

Cold Pickled Chicken

Escabeche de Gallina   *To serve 4 to 6*

⅓ cup olive oil

A 3- to 3½-pound chicken, cut into 6 to 8 serving pieces

1 cup dry white wine

1 cup distilled white vinegar

1 cup hot water

2 medium onions, peeled, halved and cut in wedges ⅛ inch thick

3 carrots, scraped and cut diagonally into slices ⅛ inch thick

1 small leek, including 1 inch of the green, washed thoroughly and cut into rounds ⅛ inch thick

1 tablespoon salt

A bouquet of 1 celery top, 2 parsley sprigs, 2 bay leaves, 2 whole cloves and ¼ teaspoon thyme, wrapped together in cheesecloth

1 lemon, cut lengthwise into halves and then crosswise into ⅛-inch slices

1. In a heavy flameproof 4- to 5-quart casserole, heat the olive oil, tipping the casserole to coat the bottom evenly and turning the heat down to moderate if the oil begins to smoke.

2. Wash the chicken pieces quickly under cold running water, pat them dry with paper towels and brown them in the oil, a few pieces at a time. Start the pieces skin side down and turn them with tongs.

3. Add the wine, vinegar, water, onions, carrots, leek, salt and bouquet, and bring to a boil over high heat.

4. Reduce the heat to low, cover the casserole, and simmer undisturbed for 30 minutes, or until the chicken is tender but not falling apart.

5. Remove the bouquet, and arrange the chicken pieces in a deep serving dish just large enough to hold them snugly in one layer.

6. Pour the cooking liquid with the vegetables over the chicken.

7. Decorate the top with the lemon slices, and cool to room temperature.

8. Cover the dish and refrigerate for at least 6 hours, or until the cooking liquids have jelled.

9. Serve on chilled plates, as the first or the main course.

Filipino Stuffed Chicken

Pollo Relleno   *To serve 8 to 10*

THE CHICKEN
Two 6-pound roasting chickens
½ cup lime or lemon juice
½ cup soy sauce
3 pounds ground pork
**4 Spanish or Italian sausages, finely
  chopped**
1 cup grated Edam or Cheddar cheese
5 eggs, lightly beaten
1½ teaspoons salt
1½ teaspoons black pepper
4 hard-cooked eggs, quartered
1 pound ham, cut into strips
4 sweet pickles, cut into strips
6 cups chicken stock
Vegetable oil for deep frying

1. Have your butcher bone the chickens, but leave the wings and legs intact.
2. Brush with a mixture of the lime juice and soy sauce.
3. Let them stand 1 hour, brushing them occasionally with the marinade, then drain them.
4. Mix together the pork, the sausages, cheese, eggs, salt and pepper. Stuff each chicken with this mixture, then press 2 hard-cooked eggs, half the ham and 2 pickles into the center of the stuffing of each.
5. Skewer the openings of the chickens.
6. Place in a large Dutch oven.
7. Add the stock, bring to a boil, cover and cook over low heat 2 hours, turning the chickens carefully once or twice.
8. Remove them, drain them well. Reserve the liquid.
9. Heat the oil to 375° and fry one chicken at a time until it is entirely browned. Drain again and keep hot.
10. To serve the chickens, slice them and then place the pieces on a platter and cover them with garlic sauce (*below*).

GARLIC SAUCE
3 tablespoons lard or butter
2 cloves garlic, minced
3 tablespoons flour
3 cups reserved liquid from chickens
2 tablespoons soy sauce

1. Melt the lard or butter in a saucepan; sauté the garlic until browned.
2. Blend in the flour, then add the reserved liquid and soy sauce, stirring steadily to the boiling point.
3. Cook over low heat 10 minutes, stirring occasionally.

Chicken with Stuffed Peppers

Poularde Andalouse   *To serve 4*

CHICKEN
A 4- to 4½-pound chicken
1 small sliced onion
1 small sliced carrot
1 sliced stalk celery
1 bay leaf
Salt
Pepper

1. Truss the chicken and place it in a heavy pot with the sliced onion, carrot and celery. Just cover with cold water and bring slowly to a boil.
2. Add the bay leaf, salt and pepper and simmer for 1 to 1¼ hours, or until the chicken is tender.
3. Meanwhile, prepare the eggplant, stuffed peppers and the sauce.

EGGPLANT
4 slices eggplant, ½ inch thick
Salt
Flour
1 large clove garlic, crushed
¼ cup olive oil

1. Sprinkle the eggplant slices with salt and let them stand for ½ hour.
2. Dry the slices with a paper towel, dust them lightly with flour and spread them with the crushed garlic.
3. Sauté the slices in hot oil until they are golden brown on both sides.
4. Keep warm.

STUFFED PEPPERS
4 green peppers
¼ cup olive oil
¼ cup chopped onion
4 small garlic sausages, chopped
¾ cup raw rice
1½ cups chicken stock
Salt
Pepper

1. Cover the green peppers with cold water, bring to a boil, simmer for 5 minutes and drain.
2. Cut off the caps, remove all seeds and set aside.
3. Heat the olive oil in a skillet. Add the chopped onion and garlic sausages and cook 3 to 4 minutes.
4. Add the raw rice and cook another 2 to 3 minutes. Cover with the chicken stock, bring to a boil and season with salt and pepper.
5. Cover and cook slowly for 20 minutes.
6. Stuff mixture into peppers and keep warm.

SAUCE
3 tablespoons butter
3 tablespoons flour
1 cup chicken stock
½ cup cream
2 pimientos, minced

1. Melt 2 tablespoons of the butter in a small saucepan. Blend in, off the fire, the flour.
2. Add the chicken stock and stir over the fire until the sauce comes to a boil.
3. Add the cream, pimientos and the remaining butter, bit by bit.

TO ASSEMBLE: 1. Remove the chicken from the pot. Carefully take off skin and cut the chicken into serving pieces.
2. Arrange them on a hot serving dish and cover with the sauce.
3. Surround with the eggplant topped with the peppers.

Roast Chicken Stuffed with Shrimp

Gefüllte Hühner mit Garnelen   *To serve 4*

A 4½- to 5-pound roasting chicken
1 teaspoon salt
½ teaspoon dried marjoram

THE STUFFING
8 slices day-old white bread
1 cup heavy cream
12 tablespoons (1½ quarter-pound sticks)
  unsalted butter, melted
2 egg yolks
8 large shrimp, cooked, shelled and
  coarsely chopped
4 large shrimp, uncooked, shelled and fine-
  ly chopped or puréed in a blender
¼ cup finely chopped parsley
¼ cup cooked green peas, fresh, frozen or
  canned
½ teaspoon salt
Freshly ground black pepper
2 egg whites
½ cup chicken stock, fresh or canned
  (optional)

1. Preheat the oven to 350°.
2. Wash the chicken quickly under cold running water, pat it dry with paper towels, then rub the inside of it with a mixture of the salt and the marjoram.
3. Toast the bread in the upper third of the oven for 5 to 8 minutes, or until it is dry but not brown.
4. Crumble it and soak it in the cream in a mixing bowl for about 5 minutes.
5. In an 8-inch saucepan, combine the bread-and-cream mixture with 4 tablespoons of the melted butter, then, stirring constantly, simmer over low heat until the mixture is pasty and smooth, somewhat resembling a soft dough.
6. Remove it from the heat, let it cool for about 10 minutes, then beat in the egg yolks, one at a time, thoroughly incorporating one before adding the other.

7. Beat in the cooked shrimp, the raw shrimp purée, the parsley and the peas.
8. Add the salt and a grinding of pepper.
9. With a wire whisk or rotary or electric beater, beat the egg whites, preferably in an unlined copper bowl, until they form stiff, unwavering peaks when the beater is lifted from the bowl.
10. With a rubber spatula, fold the egg whites into the stuffing, using an under-and-over cutting motion rather than a mixing motion, until no trace of them remains.
11. Fill the breast cavity of the chicken, but don't pack it tightly – the stuffing will expand as it cooks.
12. Fold the neck skin under the chicken and secure it with several stitches of strong thread.
13. Stuff the body cavity loosely – no more than ¾ full – and close it with trussing pins or with a needle and thread.
14. Brush the chicken all over with some of the melted butter and place it on a rack in a roasting pan just large enough to hold it. Pour the rest of the butter over the breast.
15. Roast the chicken in the middle of the oven for about 1½ hours, basting it frequently with the pan juices.
16. Test for doneness by piercing a thigh with the point of a small sharp knife. If the juice that spurts out is yellow, the chicken is done. If it is pink, roast a few minutes longer and test again.
17. Remove the chicken to a heated serving platter and let it stand for about 10 minutes before carving it.
18. Skim off as much surface fat as possible, and dilute the pan juices with ½ cup of chicken stock that has been brought to a boil in the drippings.

Finnish Stuffed Chicken

Murekkeela Täytetta Kana *To serve 8 to 10*

2 roasting chickens or capons
1 tablespoon salt
¾ teaspoon black pepper
1 whole chicken breast
¾ pound ground veal
⅓ cup fresh bread crumbs
⅓ cup light cream
1 egg, beaten
1½ teaspoons salt
½ teaspoon white pepper
Dash nutmeg
2 tablespoons minced parsley
6 tablespoons melted butter
1 cup heavy cream

1. Have the chickens or capons boned.
2. Rub the fowl inside and out with the salt and black pepper. Set them aside.
3. To make the stuffing discard the skin and bones of the chicken breast and grind the meat in a food chopper.
4. Add the veal and grind again.
5. Soak the bread crumbs in the cream, then mash smooth.
6. Add to the ground meats with the egg, salt, white pepper, nutmeg, parsley and 2 tablespoons of the melted butter.
7. Stuff the chickens with the mixture and sew the openings. Tie the chickens to hold their shapes.
8. Put the chickens in a roasting pan and pour the remaining butter over them.
9. Roast in a 375° oven 2 hours, basting and turning to brown all sides.
10. Transfer the chickens to a platter and remove the strings.
11. Stir the cream into the pan juices; place over high heat and bring to a boil, scraping the bottom of browned particles.
12. Taste for seasoning and serve in a sauceboat.

Circassian Chicken

Cerkes Tavugu *To serve 12*

Two 4-pound pullets
2 quarts water
1 onion
2 stalks celery
1 carrot
1 bay leaf
2 cloves garlic
1 tablespoon salt
3 slices white bread, trimmed
1 pound shelled walnuts, finely ground
1 tablespoon paprika
⅛ teaspoon cayenne pepper

1. Clean and wash the chickens.
2. Combine in a kettle with the water, onion, celery, carrot, bay leaf and garlic.
3. Bring to a boil, cover loosely and cook over low heat 1½ hours, or until chickens are tender, adding the salt after half the cooking time.
4. Let the chickens cool in the stock, then remove the skin and bones and cut the chickens into small pieces.
5. Strain the stock and reserve.
6. Soak the bread in a little of the reserved stock, mash it smooth, then squeeze it dry.
7. Add the bread to the walnuts, then add the paprika and cayenne.
8. Put in a large bowl and, with an electric mixer or rotary beater, gradually beat in 3½ cups of the reserved stock. Beat until the mixture becomes a smooth, creamy paste. Taste for seasoning.
9. Mix 1 cup of the sauce with the chicken pieces, then arrange on a serving dish.
10. Cover evenly with the remaining sauce. Sprinkle with paprika. Chill.

Cold Chicken with Lemon-and-Cream Sauce

To serve 6 to 8

STUFFING
2 cups (1 pound) coarsely chopped pitted dried prunes
4 cups coarsely crumbled day-old homemade-type white bread
½ cup finely chopped beef suet
¼ teaspoon dried marjoram
1 teaspoon salt
½ teaspoon freshly ground black pepper
½ cup malt vinegar

1. To make the stuffing, combine the 2 cups of prunes, the crumbs, suet, marjoram, 1 teaspoon of salt and black pepper, and toss them about in a bowl with a spoon until well blended.
2. Then stir in the ½ cup of vinegar.

CHICKEN
A 5- to 6-pound roasting chicken
1 teaspoon plus 2 tablespoons salt
1 stalk celery, cut into 2-inch lengths
1 large onion, studded with 4 whole cloves
1 large bay leaf
4 parsley sprigs
3 quarts water
1 cup malt vinegar
1 tablespoon dark-brown sugar

1. Wash the chicken under cold running water and pat it completely dry inside and out with paper towels.
2. Sprinkle the cavity with 1 teaspoon of the salt and loosely spoon in the stuffing.
3. Close the opening by lacing it with skewers or by sewing it with heavy white thread. Fasten the neck skin to the back of the chicken with a skewer and truss the bird securely.
4. Place the chicken in a heavy 6- to 8-quart casserole and arrange the celery stalk, onion, bay leaf and parsley around it.

5. Pour in the water and 1 cup of vinegar, and add the remaining 2 tablespoons of salt and the brown sugar. The water should rise at least 2 inches above the chicken; add more if necessary.
6. Bring to a boil over high heat, skimming off the scum and foam as they rise to the surface.
7. Reduce the heat to low, partially cover the pot, and simmer for 1½ to 2 hours, or until the chicken is tender but not falling apart.
8. Let the chicken cool in its stock to room temperature. Then place it on a large platter and discard the stock.

SAUCE
½ cup heavy cream
4 tablespoons fresh lemon juice
2 teaspoons finely grated lemon peel
⅛ teaspoon ground thyme
A pinch of white pepper
1 tablespoon butter
1 tablespoon flour
½ cup milk

1. In a 1- to 1½-quart enameled or stainless-steel saucepan, bring the cream, lemon juice, 1 teaspoon of the grated lemon peel, the thyme and a pinch of white pepper to a simmer over low heat.
2. Simmer for 2 or 3 minutes, then strain the cream through a fine sieve set over a bowl. Set aside.
3. In a heavy 8- to 10-inch skillet, melt the butter over moderate heat. When the foam begins to subside, stir in the flour and mix thoroughly.
4. Pour in the milk and, stirring constantly with a whisk, cook over high heat until the mixture thickens slightly and comes to a boil.
5. Reduce the heat to low and simmer for about 3 minutes to remove any taste of raw flour.
6. Then stir in the strained cream and simmer just long enough to heat the sauce through.

7. Taste for seasoning and cool the sauce to room temperature.

GARNISH
Lemon quarters or slices
6 pitted prunes, cut lengthwise into halves
Parsley sprigs

1. To assemble the dish, pour the sauce over the top of the bird and sprinkle it with 1 teaspoon of grated lemon peel.
2. Arrange the lemons, prune halves and parsley sprigs attractively around the chicken, and serve at room temperature.

Chicken Tetrazzini

To serve 4 to 6

A 4-pound chicken
1 medium-sized onion, sliced
1 carrot, sliced
1 stalk celery, sliced
Salt
Pepper
Cayenne pepper
1 bay leaf
½ pound mushrooms
6 tablespoons butter
3 tablespoons flour
½ cup cream
1 egg yolk
2 tablespoons sherry
½ pound thin spaghetti
1 cup grated Parmesan cheese

1. Tie up the chicken and place in a heavy saucepan with the sliced onion, carrot and celery; season with salt, pepper, cayenne and a bay leaf.
2. Just cover the chicken with cold water and bring slowly to a boil.
3. Simmer covered for 1 to 1¼ hours, until tender.
4. Remove the chicken, reserving the stock, skin it, take the meat off the bones and cut the meat into thin strips.
5. Slice ½ pound mushrooms and cook in 2 tablespoons of butter 10 minutes over a moderate heat, until lightly browned.
6. In another pan melt 3 tablespoons of butter.
7. Off the fire blend in 3 tablespoons of flour, salt and a pinch of cayenne pepper.
8. Add 1½ cups of the reserved chicken stock and stir over the heat until the sauce comes to a boil.
9. In a separate bowl beat ½ cup cream and 1 egg yolk lightly with a fork and then add this mixture to the sauce.
10. Stir until the sauce is hot but do not let it boil again. Add 2 tablespoons sherry, the chicken and mushrooms.
11. Meanwhile, boil ½ pound thin spaghetti, in 3 to 4 quarts of salted water, until tender, following the manufacturer's directions for cooking time.
12. Drain in a colander and rinse quickly with cold water.
13. Make a ring of spaghetti in a buttered casserole that can be used for serving.
14. Place the chicken mixture in the center. Sprinkle with 1 cup grated Parmesan cheese and dot with 1 tablespoon of butter.
15. Bake in a moderate oven at 350° for 20 to 30 minutes. If the top isn't nicely browned, finish with a few seconds under the broiler and serve immediately.

NOTE: This casserole may be prepared hours ahead of time and stored in the refrigerator. To reheat, let it stand at room temperature for ½ hour, then bake it at least 30 to 40 minutes.

Casserole-roasted Chicken

Poulet en Cocotte Bonne Femme   To serve 4

A 3½- to 4-pound roasting chicken
4 tablespoons softened butter
¼ teaspoon finely chopped garlic
½ teaspoon dried thyme, crumbled
¼ pound salt pork, diced
2 cups water
5 tablespoons butter
16 peeled white onions, about 1 inch in
**   diameter**
6 peeled carrots, cut in 2-inch cylinders or
**   olive shapes**
16 one-inch potato balls, or potatoes cut
**   in 2-inch olive shapes**
Salt
Freshly ground black pepper
Bouquet garni **made of 4 parsley sprigs and**
**   1 bay leaf, tied together**

1. Preheat the oven to 350°.
2. Wash the chicken quickly under cold running water and dry it thoroughly inside and out with paper towels.
3. Cream 2 tablespoons of softened butter until it is fluffy, and beat in the garlic and thyme. Spread the seasoned butter inside the chicken.
4. Truss the chicken and rub the outside with the remaining 2 tablespoons of softened butter.
5. Blanch the salt pork dice by simmering them in 2 cups of water for 5 minutes; drain on paper towels and pat dry.
6. In a heavy, enameled oval casserole just large enough to hold the chicken comfortably, melt 1 tablespoon of butter over moderate heat and in it brown the pork dice, stirring them or shaking the casserole frequently, until they are crisp and golden.
7. Remove them with a slotted spoon and set aside to drain on paper towels.
8. In the rendered fat left in the casserole, brown the chicken on all sides.
9. Remove from heat and pour off all but a

thin film of fat from the casserole.
10. Return the chicken and the browned pork dice to it and set aside.
11. In a heavy 10- to 12-inch skillet, melt the remaining 4 tablespoons of butter over moderate heat and in it cook the onions, carrots, and potatoes, stirring frequently, for 5 minutes, or until coated with butter and lightly colored.
12. Remove the vegetables and arrange around the chicken.
13. Season with salt and pepper, add the *bouquet garni,* and cover the casserole. If the cover isn't snug, drape a piece of foil over the chicken before covering it.
14. On top of the stove, heat the casserole until the fat begins to splutter. Cook the chicken on the middle shelf of the oven, basting it every 20 minutes with the juices that will accumulate in the casserole.
15. After 1¼ hours, start testing the chicken by lifting it with a wooden spoon inserted in its tail opening. When the juices that run out are yellow, it is done.
16. To serve, transfer the chicken to a heated platter and arrange the vegetables attractively around it.
17. Discard the *bouquet garni* and skim as much surface fat as possible from the sauce left in the casserole.
18. Taste the sauce and correct the seasoning.
19. The chicken may be carved in the kitchen or at the table. Serve the sauce separately.

Jellied Chicken Loaf

To serve 8

One 5-pound chicken
6¼ cups cold water
1 small sliced onion
1 stalk sliced celery
1 sliced carrot
1 bay leaf
1 sprig fresh parsley
Salt
3 peppercorns
2 tablespoons gelatin
Parsley or watercress

1. Tie up the chicken and place it in a deep, heavy saucepan.
2. Add 6 cups of cold water and bring slowly to a boil. Skim carefully.
3. Add the onion, celery, carrot, bay leaf, parsley, salt and peppercorns.
4. Cover and simmer until the chicken is very tender and starts falling off the bones, about 1½ hours – longer if the chicken is an old fowl.
5. Remove the chicken. Strain the stock and if there is more than 4 cups, reduce it to that amount.
6. Soften the gelatin in the ¼ cup of cold water, add it to the hot stock and stir until it is dissolved.
7. Skin the chicken, take all the meat off the bones and cut it into small dice.
8. Combine the chicken and stock and taste for seasoning.
9. Pour into a loaf pan and chill in the refrigerator until set, at least 2 to 3 hours, and much longer if you wish.
10. Unmold on a silver platter. Garnish with parsley or watercress.

Spiced Chicken and Rice

To serve 8

4 whole chicken breasts
3 teaspoons salt
½ teaspoon black pepper
½ teaspoon ginger
1 clove garlic, minced
1 pound raw rice
1 teaspoon cinnamon
6 tablespoons butter
2 cardamom pods
2 cloves
2 tablespoons yoghurt
½ teaspoon cumin
½ teaspoon saffron
10 almonds
10 raisins
¼ cup sliced onions

1. Cut the chicken breasts in half through the breastbones, wash and dry.
2. Rub the breasts with a mixture of 1½ teaspoons of salt, pepper, ginger and garlic.
3. Let stand at room temperature 30 minutes.
4. Half-cook the rice with the cinnamon and remaining salt. Drain.
5. Heat 4 tablespoons of the butter in a skillet.
6. Break the cardamom pods and add the seeds and the cloves to the butter.
7. Add the chicken, brown on both sides, and then add the yoghurt.
8. Spread half the rice in a greased casserole or deep skillet. Arrange the chicken over it and cover with the remaining rice.
9. Pour the skillet liquid from the chicken on the rice and sprinkle with the cumin and saffron.
10. Place over medium heat for 5 minutes, then over low heat for 15 minutes.
11. Sauté the almonds, raisins and onions in the remaining butter until golden in color. Sprinkle on top of the rice and chicken before serving.

Meat Cakes Steamed in Banana Leaves

Hallacas Centrales   *To make about 25*

THE DOUGH

3 cups dried white corn and 6 cups of cold water, or substitute three 1-pound-13-ounce cans of hominy
½ cup lard
1 teaspoon annatto seeds
1 teaspoon salt

THE FILLING

A 1½- to 2-pound chicken, cut into quarters
2 cups cold water
½ cup olive oil
1 pound boneless loin of pork, cut into ⅓-inch cubes
1 pound beef chuck, cut into ⅓-inch cubes
1¼ cups finely chopped green peppers
1¼ cups finely chopped onions
1 tablespoon finely chopped garlic
4 medium tomatoes, peeled, seeded and coarsely chopped, or substitute 1⅓ cups chopped, drained, canned Italian plum tomatoes
6 tablespoons capers, drained and rinsed in cold water
⅓ cup sugar
1 tablespoon ground cumin seeds
1 tablespoon salt
1½ teaspoons freshly ground black pepper
½ cup finely chopped fresh parsley
¼ pound fresh pork fat, cut into ¼-inch dice
¾ cup seedless raisins
25 pimiento-stuffed olives
3 whole banana leaves plus 25 ten-inch squares of white parchment paper, or substitute 50 ten-inch squares of white parchment paper

THE DOUGH: 1. If you are using dried corn, combine it with the water in a 4-quart saucepan and bring to a boil over high heat.
2. Reduce the heat to moderate and cook, uncovered, stirring frequently, for 20 minutes.

Drain off any excess water.
3. Put the corn through the finest blade of a meat grinder and then put it through a food mill or a coarse sieve.
4. If you are using hominy, drain it well and put it through a food mill.
5. Melt ¼ cup of lard over moderate heat in a small skillet, add the annatto seeds and cook for 3 minutes.
6. Strain the lard through a sieve and discard the seeds.
7. With a spoon or your fingers, combine the remaining ¼ cup of lard with the corn.
8. Add the strained lard and 1 teaspoon salt, and knead the dough for 10 minutes, or until it is very smooth.

THE FILLING: 1. In a 4-quart saucepan, combine the chicken and 2 cups of water, and bring to a boil over high heat.
2. Reduce the heat to low, cover and cook for 30 minutes, or until the chicken is tender but not falling apart.
3. Transfer the chicken to a plate and set the stock aside for another use.
4. Remove the skin from the chicken with a small knife or your fingers. Cut or pull the meat away from the bones. Discard the bones, and cut the meat into strips ⅛ inch wide and 1 to ½ inches long.
5. In a heavy 12-inch skillet, heat the oil over high heat until a light haze forms above it.
6. Add the pork and beef cubes, and cook, stirring frequently, until the meat is lightly browned on all sides. Transfer the meat to a plate.
7. Reduce the heat to moderate, and add the green peppers, onions and garlic to the oil remaining in the pan.
8. Cook, stirring frequently, for 5 minutes, or until the vegetables are soft but not brown.
9. Add the tomatoes and cook for 15 minutes until the tomato juices evaporate and the sauce becomes a thick purée.

continued on page 57

A fresh *hallaca*, made of corn dough with a spicy chicken, beef and pork
stuffing, rests on the banana leaf in which it was tied before being steamed.

1. To assemble a *hallaca*, smooth dough onto a banana-leaf square.

2. Spread filling in the center of the flattened dough and add the garnish.

3. Fold the sides of the leaf (against) the grain) over the filling.

4. Bring the ends of the leaf up over the filling on the seam side.

5. Lap the two ends over each other to enclose the filling securely.

6. Press the seams closed gently, trying not to tear the banana leaf.

7. Center the *hallaca* on a paper square; bring two sides of paper up together.

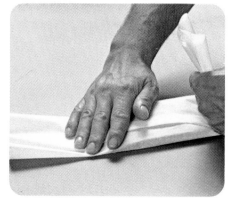

8. Make a ½-inch fold along the edge and fold again over the *hallaca*.

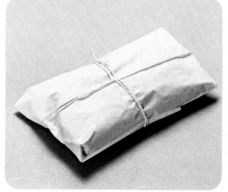

9. Close the ends over the seam side and tie snugly with kitchen cord.

10. Return the meat to the pan, add the capers, sugar, cumin, 1 tablespoon salt and black pepper, and reduce the heat to low.
11. Simmer, uncovered, stirring occasionally, for 30 minutes.
12. Stir in the chicken strips and parsley, and set the pan aside off the heat.
13. In a small skillet, cook the pork fat over moderate heat, stirring frequently, until it has rendered most of its fat. Do not let the pork brown.

TO PREPARE THE BANANA LEAVES: 1. If you are using banana leaves, cut away and discard the center ribs of the leaves with scissors, and carefully tear the leaves into 10-inch squares, following the veins of the leaf. (The leaf shreds easily if pulled against the vein.)
2. Wash the squares in cold water, rubbing them with a cloth or sponge in the direction of the vein pattern. Dry the pieces with paper towels.

TO ASSEMBLE: 1. Shape 3 tablespoons of the dough into a ball and place it in the center of a banana-leaf square or piece of parchment paper.
2. With the fingers press the dough into a rectangle about 6 inches wide and 7 inches long diagonally across the center of the leaf of paper.
3. Place 3 tablespoons of meat filling on the center of the dough and dot it with 2 or 3 pieces of pork fat, 4 or 5 raisins and 1 olive.

4. Fold one corner of the leaf (against the grain) or the paper over the filling and bring the opposite corner over on top of it. (The pictures on page 56 illustrate this process.) Bring the remaining corners up on the same side and lap them over each other to enclose the filling securely.
5. Press all the sides down gently, trying not to tear the banana leaf if you are using one.
6. Center the *hallaca* on a paper square and bring the edges of two opposite sides of the paper together above the *hallaca*
7. Make a ½-inch fold along the two edges, then press the fold down over the *hallaca*
8. Bring the open ends down over the seam side and tie the finished *hallaca* snugly with kitchen cord.

TO COOK: 1. When all the *hallacas* are filled, wrapped and tied, place them seam side down in several layers in a large colander.
2. Place the colander in a deep pot and pour enough water into the pot to come to just below the bottom of the colander.
3. Bring the water to a boil over high heat, cover the pot and reduce the heat to low.
4. Steam the *hallacas* for 1 hour, keeping the water at a slow boil and replenishing it with additional boiling water as it cooks away.
5. With kitchen tongs, transfer the *hallacas* to a heated platter.
6. They may be served at once or refrigerated overnight with no loss of flavor. Reheat by steaming them again for 30 minutes.

Chicken Pancakes

To serve 4

FRENCH PANCAKES
1½ cups flour
½ teaspoon salt
2 tablespoons sugar
1¼ teaspoons baking soda
2 cups sour milk (*see note*)
1 tablespoon melted butter
1 egg, well beaten
A piece of fat salt pork

NOTE: To make sour milk add 1½ tablespoons lemon juice or vinegar to each cupful of lukewarm sweet milk. Let stand a few minutes.

1. Sift together the flour, salt, sugar and soda. Stir in the sour milk, butter and egg.
2. Heat a griddle or heavy frying pan. Grease the pan with the salt pork, rubbing it again after each batch.
3. Drop enough batter from the tip of a spoon to make a 5-inch pancake.
4. When the cakes are puffed and full of bubbles and the edges are cooked well, turn them and cook the other side.
5. Set each one aside on a heated platter and proceed with the next one, until all the batter is used.

FILLING AND SAUCE
4 cups chicken stock
10 tablespoons butter
8 tablespoons flour
2 teaspoons salt
3 cups cooked diced chicken
1 cup sliced mushrooms
½ cup light cream
Grated Parmesan cheese

1. Heat the stock.
2. In another saucepan blend 8 tablespoons of the butter with the flour and salt.
3. Slowly add the heated stock and cook until the mixture thickens, stirring constantly.

4. Pour half the sauce into another pan and reserve it. To the remaining half add the diced chicken and mix well.
5. Melt the remaining butter in a frying pan, add the mushrooms and cook them slowly until they are nicely browned but not crisp. Add them to the reserved chicken sauce, then mix in the light cream.
6. Drop a tablespoonful of the filling in the center of each pancake. Roll the pancake up and place it with the edges down in an oven-proof baking dish.
7. Spoon the mushroom sauce over the pancakes, sprinkle them with grated Parmesan cheese and place under the broiler until they are lightly browned.

Chicken in Tortillas with Green Tomato Sauce

Enchiladas Verdes   *To serve 6*

2 whole chicken breasts, each about ¾
  pound
1 cup chicken stock, fresh or canned
6 ounces cream cheese
2 cups heavy cream
¾ cup finely chopped onions
6 fresh *poblano* chilies, about 5 inches
  long, or substitute 6 fresh green peppers,
  about 3½ inches in diameter
A 10-ounce can Mexican green tomatoes,
  drained
2 canned *serrano* chilies, drained, rinsed in

cold water and finely chopped
5 teaspoons coarsely chopped fresh
coriander (*cilantro*)
1 egg
1½ teaspoons salt
¼ teaspoon freshly ground black pepper
3 tablespoons lard
12 tortillas
⅓ cup freshly grated Parmesan cheese

NOTE: Wear rubber gloves when handling the hot chilies.

1. Place the chicken breasts in a heavy 2- to 3-quart saucepan, pour in the stock and bring to a boil over high heat.

2. Then reduce the heat to its lowest point, cover the pan, and simmer the breasts for about 20 minutes, or until they are tender but not falling apart.

3. Transfer the breasts to a plate and reserve the stock.

4. When the chicken is cool enough to handle, remove the skin, cut the meat away from the bones and shred it into small pieces.

5. In a large mixing bowl, beat the cream cheese with a wooden spoon until it is smooth, then beat into it ½ cup of cream, 3 tablespoons at a time. Stir in the onions, add the shredded chicken, mix thoroughly, and put the mixture aside while you make the sauce.

6. Roast the *poblano* chilies or green peppers by impaling them, one at a time, on the tines of a long-handled fork and turning them over a gas flame until the skin blisters and darkens on all sides. Or place the chilies on a baking sheet or broiler pan, and broil them about 3 inches from the heat for about 5 minutes or so, turning them so that they color on all sides. Be careful not to let them burn.

7. Wrap the chilies in a damp, clean towel and let them rest in the towel for a few minutes.

8. Gently rub them with the towel until the skins slip off.

9. Cut out their stems and thick white mem-branes, and discard the seeds.

10. Chop the chilies coarsely and place them in the jar of an electric blender.

11. Add the tomatoes, *serrano* chilies, coriander and ¼ cup of the reserved chicken stock.

12. Blend at high speed until the mixture is reduced to a smooth purée.

13. Pour in the remaining 1½ cups of cream, the egg, salt and pepper, and blend for 10 seconds longer.

14. Scrape the purée into a large bowl. (To make the sauce by hand, purée the chilies, tomatoes, *serrano* chilies and coriander in a food mill set over a bowl. Discard any pulp remaining in the mill. Stir in the ¼ cup of stock, 1½ cups of cream, the egg, salt, and pepper, and mix together thoroughly.)

15. Preheat the oven to 350°.

16. In a heavy 8- to 10-inch skillet, melt the lard over moderate heat until a light haze forms above it.

17. Fry and fill the tortillas, one at a time, in the following traditional fashion: Dip a tortilla in the chili-tomato sauce, drop it into the skillet and fry it for a minute or so on each side, or until limp.

18. Transfer the tortilla from the pan to a plate and place ¼ cup of the chicken filling in its center.

19. Fold one side of the tortilla over the filling, then roll the tortilla up completely into a thick cylinder. Place it, seam side down, in a shallow 8-by-12-inch baking dish.

20. Fry and fill the remaining tortillas in a similar fashion, replenishing the lard in the frying pan when necessary.

21. When the tortillas are all arranged in one layer in the baking dish, pour the remaining chili-tomato sauce over them and sprinkle the top evenly with grated cheese.

22. Bake on the middle shelf of the oven for about 15 minutes, or until the cheese melts and the enchiladas brown lightly on top. Serve at once.

Chicken in Cornhusks

Tamales   *To make 24 tamales*

**24 dried cornhusks, or substitute 24 sheets
  of baking parchment paper, 4 by 9 inches**
⅓ cup lard
2 cups instant *masa harina* (corn flour)
2 teaspoons double-acting baking powder
1½ teaspoons salt
**1½ cups lukewarm beef or chicken stock,
  fresh or canned**

THE FILLING
**1½ cups *pollo en adobo (below)*, cut in
  ¼-inch dice and moistened with its sauce**

1. In a large bowl or pot, cover the cornhusks
(if you are using them) with hot water and
let them soak for 30 minutes. Then drain and
pat the husks dry with paper towels.
2. Meanwhile, cream the lard with an electric beater at medium speed for 10 minutes,
or beat and mash it against the sides of a bowl
with a spoon for about 20 minutes, or until
light and fluffy.
3. In another bowl, mix the *masa harina,* baking powder and salt together, then beat it
about ¼ cup at a time into the creamed lard,
continuing to beat until the ingredients are
thoroughly combined.
4. Slowly pour in the lukewarm stock, stirring constantly; beat for 4 or 5 minutes until
a soft, moist dough is formed.
5. Assemble the tamales one at a time in the
following fashion: Place about a tablespoon
of dough in the center or a cornhusk or sheet
of paper and, with a knife or metal spatula,
spread it into a rectangle about 3 inches by
nearly 4 inches to reach almost to the long
sides of the husk or paper.
6. Drop a heaping tablespoon of filling in the
center of the dough. Then fold one side of
the wrapper a little more than halfway across
the filling and bring the opposite side over the
first fold.
7. Turn the ends up to cover the seam,

overlapping them across the top.
8. Lay the tamales, seam side down, in a
large colander in as many layers as necessary.
9. Place the colander in a deep pot about 1
inch larger in diameter than the colander, and
pour enough water into the pot to come to
an inch below the bottom of the colander.
10. Bring the water to a vigorous boil over
high heat, cover the pot securely and reduce
the heat to low.
11. Steam the tamales for an hour, keeping
the water at a slow boil and replenishing it
with boiling water as it evaporates.
12. When the tamales are done, remove
them from the colander with tongs, arrange
them on a heated platter and serve at once.
The tamales may be cooked ahead if you like
and reheated by steaming them again for half
an hour.

POLLO EN ADOBO
6 dried *ancho* chilies
**1 cup boiling chicken stock, fresh or
  canned**
1 cup coarsely chopped onions
**3 medium tomatoes, peeled, seeded and
  coarsely chopped, or substitute**
**1 cup drained, canned Italian plum
  tomatoes**
1 teaspoon finely chopped garlic
1 tablespoon white vinegar
1 teaspoon sugar
½ teaspoon ground coriander seeds
¼ teaspoon ground cinnamon
¼ teaspoon ground cloves
1½ teaspoons salt
¼ teaspoon freshly ground black pepper
4 tablespoons lard
**A 3- to 3½-pound chicken, cut into 6 or 8
  serving pieces**

NOTE: Wear rubber gloves when handling the
hot chilies.
1. Under cold running water, pull the stems
off the chilies, break them in half, and brush
out the seeds.
2. With a small, sharp knife, cut away any

Dried cornhusks are the traditional wrapper for the Mexican tamale – shown
freshly cooked, in a basket, and newly opened and ready to eat, on a plate.

large ribs.
3. Tear the chilies into small pieces, pour 1 cup of boiling stock over them and let them soak for 30 minutes.
4. Pour the chilies and the stock into the jar of a blender and purée at high speed for about 15 seconds.
5. Add the onions, tomatoes, garlic, vinegar, sugar, coriander, cinnamon, cloves, salt and black pepper, and blend for 30 seconds, or until the mixture is reduced to a thick purée.
6. In a heavy 8-inch skillet, heat 1 tablespoon of the lard over moderate heat.
7. Add the purée and cook, uncovered, stirring occasionally, for 5 minutes.
8. Remove from the heat; cover the skillet to keep the sauce warm.
9. Preheat the oven to 350°.
10. Pat the chicken pieces dry with paper towels (they will not brown well if they are damp).
11. In a heavy 10- to 12-inch skillet melt the remaining 3 tablespoons of lard over moderate heat until a light haze forms above it.
12. Brown the chicken a few pieces at a time, starting them skin side down and turning them with tongs. As the pieces turn a rich golden brown, place them in a 3-quart heatproof casserole.
13. Pour the chili sauce into the casserole and turn the chicken about in it until the pieces are thoroughly coated with the sauce.
14. Cover the casserole tightly and bake, undisturbed, in the middle of the oven for 45 minutes.
15. Then remove the cover and bake 15 minutes longer, basting the chicken evey now and then with its sauce.

Mexican Chicken in Pastry Shells

Pastel de Mole   *To serve 12*

1 can *mole poblano*
3 tablespoons olive oil
¾ cup peeled, seeded, chopped tomatoes
1 teaspoon sugar
2 cups chicken broth
3 cups diced cooked chicken or turkey
12 heated patty shells

NOTE: *Mole poblano* is available in Mexican, Spanish or specialty shops.
1. Heat the oil in a saucepan, stir in the *mole* and cook, stirring almost constantly, for 2 minutes.
2. Add the tomatoes and sugar; cook over low heat for 3 minutes.
3. Gradually add the broth, stirring constantly.
4. Cook over low heat for 20 minutes.
5. Mix in the chicken and cook 5 minutes longer.
6. Fill the shells and serve immediately.

Chicken and Leek Pie

To serve 4 to 6

PUFF PASTRY
2 cups sifted all-purpose flour
¼ teaspoon salt
¼ pound (1 stick) unsalted butter, cut into ¼-inch bits and thoroughly chilled
¼ cup lard, cut in ¼-inch bits and thoroughly chilled
4 to 6 tablespoons ice water

1. Sift the flour and salt together into a large chilled mixing bowl.
2. Drop in the butter and lard and, working quickly, use your fingertips to rub the flour and fat together until the mixture looks like flakes of coarse meal.
3. Pour 4 tablespoons of ice water over the mixture all at once, and gather the dough into a ball.
4. If the dough crumbles, add up to 2 tablespoons more ice water, 1 teaspoon at a time, until the particles adhere.
5. Dust lightly with flour, wrap the dough in wax paper and chill for 30 minutes.
6. Place the pastry on a lightly floured board or table, and press it into a rectangular shape about 1 inch thick.
7. Dust a little flour over and under it, and roll it out into a strip about 21 inches long and 6 inches wide.
8. Fold the strip into thirds to form a 3-layered rectangular packet, reducing its dimensions to about 7 by 6 inches.
9. Turn the pastry around so that an open end faces you and roll it out once more to a 21-by-6-inch strip.
10. Fold it into thirds as before and roll it out again to a similar strip.
11. Repeat this entire process twice more, end-

ing with the pastry folded into a packet.

12. Wrap the pastry tightly in wax paper, foil or a plastic bag, and refrigerate it for at least 1 hour. It may be kept in the refrigerator for 3 or 4 days.

FILLING

A 4- to 4½-pound roasting chicken or
   stewing fowl
1 large onion, peeled and quartered
1 small celery stalk including the leaves
A bouquet of 8 parsley sprigs and 1 small
   bay leaf, tied together
¼ teaspoon thyme
1 tablespoon salt
10 medium-sized leeks, including 1 inch of
   the green stems, split in half and cut
   crosswise into 1-inch pieces
¼ pound cooked smoked beef tongue, cut
   into ⅛-inch slices
1 tablespoon finely chopped parsley
1 egg yolk combined with 1 tablespoon
   heavy cream
¼ cup heavy cream

1. In a heavy 6- to 8-quart pot, combine the chicken or fowl, onion, celery stalk, bouquet of parsley and bay leaf, thyme and salt, and pour in enough cold water to cover the chicken by 1 inch.

2. Bring to a boil over high heat, meanwhile skimming off all the foam and scum with a large spoon as they rise to the surface.

3. Then reduce the heat to low and simmer partially covered until the bird is tender but not falling apart. (A roasting chicken should be done in about 1 hour; a stewing fowl may take as long as 2 hours or more.)

4. Transfer the chicken to a plate and strain the stock through a fine sieve set over a bowl, pressing down hard on the vegetables and herbs with the back of a spoon before discarding them.

5. Pour 2 cups of the stock into a heavy 2- to 3-quart saucepan and skim the surface of its fat.

6. Add the leeks and bring to a boil over high heat.

7. Then reduce the heat to low and simmer partially covered for 15 minutes, or until the leeks are tender.

8. With a small, sharp knife, remove the skin from the chicken and cut the meat away from the bones.

9. Discard the skin and bones, cut the meat into 1-inch pieces, arrange them evenly on the bottom of a 1½-quart caserole or baking dish at least 2 inches deep.

10. Pour the leeks and their stock over the chicken and sprinkle lightly with salt.

11. Arrange the slices of tongue side by side over the top, but leave a space about 1 inch square in the center.

12. Sprinkle with the chopped parsley.

13. Preheat the oven to 400°

14. On a lightly floured surface roll out the puff pastry into a rough rectangle about ¼ inch thick. Then cut 2 strips, each about 12 inches long and ½ inch wide, from the ends.

15. Lay the strips end to end around the rim of the baking dish and press them firmly into place. Moisten them lightly with a pastry brush dipped in cold water.

16. Drape the remaining pastry over the rolling pin, lift it up, and unfold it over th baking dish. Trim off the excess with a small, sharp knife and, with the tines of a fork or your fingers, crimp the pastry to secure it to the rim.

17. Gather the scraps of pastry into a ball, reroll and cut them into simple leaf and flower shapes; moisten one side with the egg-yolk-and-cream mixture and arrange them decoratively on the pie.

18. Then brush the entire pastry surface with the remaining egg-yolk-and-cream mixture and cut a 1-inch round hold in the center of the pie.

19. Bake the pie in the middle of the oven for 1 hour, or until the crust is golden brown.

20. Just before serving, heat the ¼ cup of cream to lukewarm and pour it through the hole in the crust.

Spanish Chicken Pie

Empanada Gallega   *To serve 4 to 6*

BREAD DOUGH

1 package or cake of active dry or
   compressed yeast
½ teaspoon sugar
½ cup lukewarm water (100° to 115°)
2½ to 3 cups all-purpose flour
1½ teaspoons salt
½ cup lukewarm milk (100° to 115°)
1 tablespoon olive oil
1 egg, lightly beaten

1. In a small bowl, sprinkle the yeast and sugar over ¼ cup of the lukewarm water. Let it stand for 2 or 3 minutes, then stir to dissolve the yeast completely. Set the bowl in a warm, draft-free place, such as an unlighted oven, for 8 to 10 minutes, or until the mixture doubles in volume.

2. Combine 2 cups of the flour and the salt in a deep mixing bowl, make a well in the center, and pour in the yeast, milk and remaining ¼ cup of lukewarm water.

3. Slowly stir together, adding up to 1 cup more flour, a few tablespoons at a time, until the mixture becomes a medium-firm dough that can be lifted up in a moist, solid mass.

4. Place the dough on a lightly floured surface and knead it by pressing down, pushing it forward several times with the heel of your hand.

5. Fold it back on itself and knead for at least 10 minutes, or until the dough is smooth and elastic. Sprinkle a little flour over and under the dough when necessary to prevent it from sticking to the board.

6. Gather the dough into a ball and place it in a large, lightly buttered bowl. Dust the top with flour, drape a towel over it, and set in the warm place for 1½ hours or until the dough doubles in bulk.

7. Punch it down with one blow of your fist, cover with a towel and let it rise again for 45 minutes.

FILLING

A 2- to 2½-pound chicken, cut into 6 to 8
   serving pieces
1 large onion, quartered
3 tablespoons olive oil
½ cup finely chopped onions
½ teaspoon finely chopped garlic
1 medium-sized sweet red or green pepper,
   deribbed, seeded and cut into ¼-inch
   squares
½ cup finely chopped *serrano* ham or
   substitute prosciutto or other lean smoked
   ham 3 medium-sized tomatoes peeled,
   seeded and finely chopped, or substitute
   1 cup chopped, drained, canned
   tomatoes
½ teaspoon salt
¼ teaspoon freshly ground black pepper

To prepare the filling: 1. Place the chicken and quartered onion in a 3- to 4-quart saucepan and add enough water to cover them by 1 inch. Bring to a boil over high heat, meanwhile skimming off the foam and scum as they rise to the surface.

2. Reduce the heat to low, cover and cook the chicken for 30 minutes or until tender but not falling apart.

3. Transfer the chicken to a plate.

4. When the chicken is cool enough to handle, remove the skin with a small knife or your fingers. Cut or pull the meat away from the bones.

5. Discard the skin and bones, and cut the chicken meat into ½-inch cubes. Set aside.

6. In a 10- to 12-inch skillet, heat 2 tablespoons of the olive oil over moderate heat until a light haze forms above it.

7. Add the onions, garlic and red or green pepper and, stirring frequently, cook for 8 to 10 minutes, or until the vegetables are soft but not brown.

8. Stir in the ham, then add the tomatoes, raise the heat and cook briskly until most of the liquid in the pan evaporates and the mixture is thick enough to hold its shape lightly in a spoon.

This hearty meat pie, called an *empanada*, brims with a savory mixture of chicken, onions and sweet pepper. It is popular in Spain and Latin America.

9. Add the chicken, salt and pepper, taste for seasoning and cool to room temperature.
10. Preheat the oven to 375°.
11. With a pastry brush, coat a large baking sheet with the remaining tablespoon of olive oil.

To assemble the pie: 1. Divide the dough into halves.
2. On a lightly floured surface, roll each half into a circle about 12 inches in a diameter and ¼-inch thick.
3. Place one of the circles on the baking sheet and spoon the filling on top, spreading it to within about 1 inch of the outside edges.
4. Place the second circle of dough over the filling, pressing it down firmly around the edges.
5. Then fold up the entire rim of the pie by about ½ inch and press all around the outer edges with your fingertips or the tines of a fork to seal them securely.
6. Let the pie rise in the warm place for about 20 minutes.
7. Brush the pie with the beaten egg and bake in the middle of the oven for 45 minutes, or until the top is golden.
8. Serve hot, or at room temperature.

Old-fashioned Chicken Pie

To serve 6 to 8

PASTRY
1¼ cups flour
4 tablespoons vegetable shortening or lard
2 tablespoons chilled butter, cut in ¼-inch pieces
⅛ teaspoons salt
3 tablespoons ice water

1. In a large mixing bowl, combine the flour, vegetable shortening or lard, butter and salt.
2. Working quickly, use your fingertips to rub flour and fat together until they look like flakes of coarse meal.
3. Pour the ice water over the mixture, toss together, and press and knead gently with your hands until the dough can be gathered into a compact ball.
4. Dust very lightly with flour, wrap in wax paper and chill for at least ½ hour, or until you are about to make the pie.

A 5-pound roasting chicken, securely trussed
4 quarts chicken stock, fresh or canned, or half chicken stock and half water combined
½ teaspoon salt
12 to 16 small white onions, peeled, about 1 inch in diameter
4 large carrots, scraped and sliced, about 1 inch thick
8 tablespoons butter (1 quarter-pound stick), cut into small pieces
⅔ cup flour
½ cup heavy cream
1 tablespoon melted, cooled cutter

1. Place the chicken in an 8-quart soup pot and cover it with the chicken stock or chicken stock and water. Add the ½ teaspoon of salt and bring the stock to a boil over high heat.
2. Skim off all scum and froth as it rises to the surface.

3. Partially cover the pan, reduce the heat to low and simmer the chicken, undisturbed, for about 1½ hours, or until tender but not falling apart.
4. Remove the chicken and set it aside to cool.
5. Meanwhile, add the peeled onions and sliced carrots to the stock. Simmer, half covered, for about 20 minutes, or until the vegetables can be easily pierced with the point of a small, sharp knife.
6. Remove them with a slotted spoon to a small bowl.
7. Carefully remove and discard the skin from the chicken and cut the meat away from the bones.
8. Cut the pieces into 1½-to 2-inch chunks.
9. Off the heat, stir in the flour and mix until smooth.
10. Skim the fat from the stock, then, in a slow stream pour 5 cups into the saucepan, stirring with a whisk all the while.
11. Return the pan to moderate heat to cook, whisking constantly, until the sauce is thick and smooth.
12. Stir in the cream and taste for seasoning.
13. Preheat the oven to 375°.
14. Pour the sauce into a baking dish approximately 9 by 12 by 2 inches.
15. Add the chicken, onions and carrots, and spread them out evenly.
16. Then roll the dough on a lightly floured surface into a rectangle about 10 by 13 inches. Lift it up on a rolling pin and drape it over the top of the pan.
17. Crimp the pastry around the sides of the pan to seal and secure it, and brush it with the tablespoons of melted butter.
18. Make 2 small slits in the pastry to allow the steam to escape. Bake the pie in the middle of the oven for about 45 minutes, or until the crust is golden brown.

Chicken Pie

To serve 5 or 6

A 4- to 4½-pound chicken
1 small onion, sliced
1 carrot, sliced
1 stalk celery, sliced
1 bay leaf
Salt
Peppercorns
4 tablespoons butter
4 tablespoons flour
1½ cups chicken stock
½ cup light cream
1 tablespoon grated Parmesan cheese
¼ pound mushrooms, sliced and sauteed
4 hard-cooked eggs, cut in eighths
1 egg, lightly beaten

1. Tie up the chicken and place it in a deep, heavy saucepan. Barely cover it with cold water and bring slowly to a boil.
2. Skim the stock. Add the onion, carrot, celery, bay leaf, salt and a few peppercorns.
3. Cover and simmer about 1 to 1¼ hours, until the chicken is tender. If there is time, cool the chicken in the water it was cooked in.

QUICK PUFF CRUST
2 cups flour
1 teaspoon salt
1½ sticks butter (¼ pound each)
¼ cup ice water

QUICK PUFF CRUST: 1. Put the flour on a cool board or marble slab. Make a well in the center and in it put the salt and the butter. Work the ice water, bit by bit, into the butter.
2. Cover with the flour and work quickly together with the heel of your hand. Knead lightly for a few seconds.
3. Wrap in waxed paper and chill in the refrigerator for at least ½ hour before rolling out.

ASSEMBLY: 1. Remove the chicken from the stock. Skin and bone it and cut the meat into coarse shreds.
2. Melt the butter. Remove from the heat and blend in the flour.
3. Add 1½ cups of the strained chicken stock and stir over the fire until the sauce comes to a boil.
4. Add the light cream and the grated Parmesan cheese. Taste for seasoning.
5. Put all but ½ cup of the shredded chicken into the sauce with the sautéed mushrooms and hard-cooked eggs.
6. Place in a deep 9-inch pie plate.
7. Put the ½ cup of chicken over the sauce – this keeps the sauce from coming into direct contact with the crust and prevents sogginess.
8. Brush the edge of the dish with beaten egg.
9. Roll out the crust and place over the filling. Decorate with small fluted rounds of crust.
10. Pierce several times with a fork for steam to escape. Brush the top with beaten egg.
11. Chill in the refrigerator for at least ½ hour, or as long as you wish.
12. Preheat the oven to 375° and bake for 30 to 35 minutes, until golden brown.
13. Serve in the pie dish.

Chicken and Ham Pie

To serve 10 to 12

PASTRY
3 cups flour
1 teaspoon salt
1 cup shortening
2 egg yolks
⅓ cup ice water

1. Sift the flour and salt into a bowl; cut in the shortening with a pastry blender or two knives.
2. Beat the egg yolks with the water and add, tossing until a ball of dough is formed.
3. Wrap in foil or waxed paper and chill while preparing the chicken.

CHICKEN
2 3-pound chickens, disjointed
½ cup flour
4 teaspoons salt
¾ teaspoon black pepper
4 tablespoons butter
1½ quarts water
4 tablespoons tapioca
4 cloves and 4 peppercorns, tied in cheesecloth
A dash of cayenne pepper
¼ teaspoon mace
½ pound cooked ham, cubed
3 hard-cooked eggs, sliced
2 raw egg yolks, beaten

1. Wash and dry the chicken pieces, then roll in a mixture of the flour, 3 teaspoons of the salt and ½ teaspoon pepper.
2. Melt the butter in a large deep skillet; brown the chicken in it.
3. Add the water and bring to a boil.
4. Mix in the tapioca and remaining salt and pepper, then add the spice bag, cayenne and mace.
5. Cook over low heat for 45 minutes, or until chicken is tender.
6. Remove the chicken and cut the meat from the bones. Discard the spice bag. Taste the broth and season, if necessary.
7. Mix the cut-up chicken with the ham and sliced eggs. Cool.
8. Stir the broth into the beaten egg yolks, then cook, stirring steadily, until thickened, but do not let it boil. Cool.
9. Preheat the oven to 450°.
10. Divide the pastry into two pieces, one larger than the other. Roll out the larger piece and line a shallow 2-quart casserole with it.
11. Put the chicken mixture in it, and pour the thickened broth over it.
12. Cover with the remaining rolled-out pastry, sealing the edges.
13. Make a few slits in the top to allow the steam to escape.
14. Bake at 450° for 10 minutes, then reduce the heat to 350° and bake 30 minutes longer, or until browned.
15. Serve directly from the pie plate.

French Chicken Fricassee

Fricassée de Poulet à l'Ancienne　　　　*To serve 4*

A 2½- to 3-pound frying chicken, cut up
8 tablespoons butter (1 quarter-pound stick)
Salt
White pepper
¼ cup flour
3 cups hot chicken stock, fresh or canned
***Bouquet garni* made of 4 parsley sprigs and 1 bay leaf, tied together**
¼ teaspoon dried thyme, crumbled
⅔ cup chicken stock, fresh or canned
16 to 24 peeled white onions, about 1 inch in diameter
¾ pound fresh mushrooms, whole if small, sliced or quartered if large
1 teaspoon lemon juice
2 egg yolks
½ cup heavy cream
2 tablespoons finely chopped fresh parsley

1. Wash the chicken quickly under cold running water and dry the pieces thoroughly with paper towels.

2. In a heavy 2- to 3-quart flameproof casserole, melt 6 tablespoons of the butter over moderate heat.

3. Using tongs, lay a few pieces of chicken at a time in the butter and cook them, turning them once or twice, for about 5 minutes, or until they stiffen slightly and are no longer pink. Do not let them brown.

4. Remove to a plate and season with salt and white pepper.

5. With a wooden spoon, stir the flour into the butter remaining in the casserole and cook over low heat, stirring constantly, for 1 or 2 minutes without letting it brown. Remove from heat.

6. Slowly pour in the hot chicken stock, beating vigorously to blend *roux* and liquid.

7. Return to heat, whisking constantly until the sauce thickens and comes to a boil. Then reduce the heat and let the sauce simmer slowly for 1 minute.

8. Return the chicken to the casserole together with the juices that have collected on the plate, and add the *bouquet garni* and thyme. The sauce should almost cover the chicken; add more stock if it doesn't.

9. Bring to a boil, cover, reduce heat and simmer for 30 minutes.

10. Meanwhile, combine 2/3 cup stock, the remaining 2 tablespoons butter and the onions in an 8- to 10-inch enameled or stainless-steel skillet.

11. Bring to a boil, cover and simmer over low heat for 15 to 20 minutes, or until the onions are tender when pierced with the tip of a sharp knife.

12. With a slotted spoon, transfer the onions to a bowl.

13. Stir the mushrooms and lemon juice into the stock remaining in the skillet.

14. Bring to a boil, cover and simmer for 5 minutes.

15. Add the mushrooms to the onions.

16. Boil the liquid remaining in the skillet until it has reduced to 2 or 3 tablespoons, and pour it into the simmering casserole of chicken.

17. To test the chicken for doneness, pierce a thigh with the tip of a sharp knife; the juices should run pale yellow.

18. With tongs, transfer the chicken to a plate and discard the *bouquet garni.*

19. Skim the fat from the surface of the sauce, which by now should be as thick as heavy cream; if it isn't, boil the sauce rapidly, uncovered, until it reaches the desired consistency.

20. With a wire whisk blend the egg yolks and cream together in a bowl.

21. Whisk in the hot sauce, 2 tablespoons at a time, until 1/2 cup has been added; then reverse the process and whisk the egg-yolk-and-cream mixture back into the remaining hot sauce.

22. Bring it to a boil, stirring constantly, then boil slowly for 30 seconds.

23. Taste and correct the seasoning with salt, white pepper and a few drops of lemon juice.

24. Strain through a fine sieve into a large bowl.

25. Wash the casserole, arrange the chicken pieces, onions and mushrooms attractively in it, and pour the sauce over them. Do not use any juices that have accumulated under the chicken unless the sauce needs thinning.

26. Before serving, cover the casserole and simmer it over moderate heat for 5 to 10 minutes, or until the chicken is hot. Do not let the sauce come to a boil again.

27. Serve the chicken directly from the casserole or arranged on a heated platter, masked with sauce and sprinkled with parsley.

Berlin-Style Chicken Fricassee

Berliner Hühnerfrikassee   *To serve 8*

TONGUE

A 1-pound fresh veal tongue
1 medium-sized onion, peeled and quartered
A bouquet made of 2 celery tops and 2 parsley sprigs tied together
½ teaspoon salt

TONGUE: 1. In a large saucepan, combine the tongue, quartered onion, bouquet and salt. Pour in enough cold water to cover the tongue by at least 2 inches, and bring to a boil over high heat.

2. Reduce the heat to low, partially cover the pan and simmer for about 2 hours, or until the meat shows no resistance when pierced with the tip of a sharp knife. Add boiling water to the pan if needed; the tongue should be covered with water throughout the cooking period.

3. Remove the tongue from the stock and while it is still hot, skin it with a small, sharp knife, cutting away the fat, bones and gristle at its base.

4. Cut the tongue into ½-inch slices, then into ½-inch dice and set aside in a bowl.

5. Discard the cooking liquid and vegetables.

SWEETBREADS

1 pair veal sweetbreads (about ¾ pound)
Vinegar
1 teaspoon fresh lemon juice
2 teaspoons salt

SWEETBREADS: 1. Soak the sweetbreads for 2 hours in enough cold water to cover them, changing the water every 30 minutes or so.

2. Then soak them for another hour in acidulated cold water, using 1 tablespoon of vinegar for each quart of water.

3. Gently pull off as much of the outside membrane as possible without tearing the sweetbreads. Cut the two lobes of the pair of sweetbreads from the tube between them with a small, sharp knife; discard the tube.

4. Place the sweetbreads in an enameled saucepan with enough water to cover them by 2 inches, add the lemon juice and salt and bring to a boil.

5. Reduce the heat to its lowest point and simmer uncovered for 15 to 20 minutes, or until the sweetbreads are tender when pierced with the tip of a fork.

6. Drain and dry with paper towels. Then cut them into ½-inch dice and set them aside in a bowl.

CHICKEN

A 4-pound fowl or roasting chicken
2 carrots, scraped and coarsely chopped
2 leeks, including 2 inches of green, coarsely chopped
2 medium-sized onions, peeled and coarsely chopped
4 parsley sprigs
1 tablespoon salt
10 cups water

CHICKEN: 1. In a 6-quart soup pot, combine the chicken, chopped carrots, leeks, chopped onions, parsley and 1 tablespoon salt.

2. Add 10 cups of cold water, then bring to a boil over high heat, reduce the heat to low, partially cover the pot and simmer for 2½ to 3 hours if you are using a fowl, or for 1½ to 2 hours if you are using a roasting chicken.

3. When the chicken is tender but not falling apart, take it from the pot.

4. When it is cool enough to handle remove its skin with a small, sharp knife, and cut the meat away from the bones.

5. Return the skin and bones to the stock, cut the chicken meat into ½-inch dice and set aside in a bowl covered with plastic wrap.

6. Bring the stock remaining in the pot to a boil again, reduce the heat and simmer for 30 minutes longer. Then strain it through a fine sieve set over a mixing bowl and set it aside.

ASPARAGUS
1 pound fresh asparagus
2 teaspoons salt

ASPARAGUS: 1. With a small, sharp knife, cut off the butt ends of the asparagus spears and peel the tough skin from the lower end of each spear.
2. Wash the spears under cold running water and divide them into 2 equal bunches. Tie each bunch together with loops of string at each end.
3. In an enameled or stainless-steel pot large enough to hold the asparagus horizontally, bring 4 quarts of water and 2 teaspoons of salt to a bubbling boil.
4. Drop in the asparagus, bring the water to a boil, reduce the heat to moderate and cook uncovered for 8 to 10 minutes, or until the butt ends are tender but still slightly resistant when pierced with the tip of a sharp knife.
5. With two kitchen forks, lift the bundles out of the water by their strings and drain them on paper towels. Cut the stalks into 1-inch lengths and set aside.

SHRIMP
1 pound raw shrimp in their shells (about 26 to 30 per pound)
1 teaspoon salt

SHRIMP: 1. Shell the shrimp, and with a small, sharp knife, make a shallow incision down the back of each shrimp and lift out the black or white intestinal vein.
2. Wash the shrimp under cold running water.
3. Bring 2 quarts of water and 1 teaspoon salt to a boil in a 3- to 4-quart saucepan.
3. Drop in the shrimp, reduce the heat to moderate and boil uncovered for 3 to 4 minutes, or until the shrimp turn pink and are firm. Do not overcook.
4. Drain and set them aside.

MUSHROOMS
½ pound small fresh mushrooms, trimmed and sliced thinly
1 teaspoon salt
1 teaspoon fresh lemon juice

MUSHROOMS: 1. Wipe the mushrooms with a damp paper towel and cut away the tough ends of the mushroom stems.
2. Bring 3 cups of water, 1 teaspoon salt and 1 teaspoon of lemon juice to a boil in a 2- to 3-quart enameled or stainless-steel saucepan and drop in the mushrooms.
3. Reduce the heat to low, cover and simmer for about 3 minutes.
4. Drain thoroughly, let the mushrooms cool, and chop them into fine dice. Set aside.

SAUCE
6 tablespoons butter
6 tablespoons flour
3 egg yolks
3 tablespoons fresh lemon juice

SAUCE: 1. Skim the fat from the surface of the reserved chicken stock.
2. In a 2-quart enameled or stainless-steel saucepan, melt 6 tablespoons of butter over moderate heat. When the foam subsides, stir in the flour.
3. Pour in 6 cups of the stock and, beating vigorously with a whisk, bring the sauce to a boil. When it is quite thick and smooth, reduce the heat to low and simmer slowly for 5 minutes.
4. Break up the egg yolks with a fork, then stir in ¼ cup of the simmering sauce.
5. Whisk the egg-yolk mixture into the pan and bring the sauce to a boil, over moderate heat, stirring constantly.
6. Boil for 30 seconds, remove from the heat and stir in the 3 tablespoons of lemon juice. Taste for seasoning.

continued on next page

TO ASSEMBLE: 1. In a large heavy casserole combine the sauce with the reserved tongue, sweetbreads, chicken, shrimp and mushrooms but do not include any juices which may have accumulated around them.

2. Add the asparagus, and stir together gently but thoroughly with a large spoon. Taste for seasoning.

3. Simmer over moderate heat, stirring occasionally, until the mixture is heated through.

4. Serve directly from the casserole.

German Chicken Fricassee

Hühnerfrikassee   *To serve 6 to 8*

2 four-pound chickens, cut up
1 lemon
Salt
5 cups water
¼ pound butter
4 tablespoons flour
¼ pound mushrooms, chopped
½ cup dry white wine
Pepper
3 egg yolks
⅓ cup heavy cream

1. Wash and dry the chickens.

2. Cut the lemon in two, squeeze one half, reserving the juice, and with the other rub the chicken pieces. Sprinkle them with 1½ teaspoons of salt.

3. Bring the water and another 1½ teaspoons of salt to a boil, add the chicken, and cook for 5 minutes.

4. Drain and dry the chicken, reserving the liquid.

5. Melt half the butter in a Dutch oven and lightly brown the chicken in it.

6. Add the liquid, bring to a boil, and simmer for 45 minutes, or until the chicken is tender.

7. Remove the chicken, reserving the stock. Carefully pull off the skin of the chicken.

8. Melt the remaining butter and stir in the flour.

9. Add the stock, stirring until it has thickened.

10. Add the mushrooms, wine and lemon juice, plus salt and pepper to taste. Simmer for 10 minutes.

11. Beat the egg yolks and cream together, then stir in a little of the hot sauce.

12. Return this mixture to the balance of the sauce, stirring steadily.

13. Add the chicken, and place the fricassee over the lowest possible heat until the chicken is heated through.

14. Serve at once.

Chinese Chicken Stock

Chi-t'ang   *To make about 3 quarts*

A 5-pound stewing chicken (or substitute 5 pounds chicken necks, backs or uncooked bones)
2 slices peeled fresh ginger root, each about 1 inch in diameter and ½ inch thick
1 scallion, including the green top, cut into 1-inch lengths

1. Place the chicken in a 6-quart heavy pot and pour in enough cold water to cover the chicken (about 4 quarts).

2. Drop in the ginger slices and cut-up scallions.

3. Bring the water to a boil over high heat, skim the surface of any scum or foam that rises to the top, then partially cover the pot.

4. Reduce the heat to low and simmer the chicken for about 2 hours, or until it is tender and almost falling apart.

5. Remove the chicken from the stock and set aside for another use.

6. Strain the stock through a fine sieve into a large bowl, cool, then refrigerate. The fat that will congeal on the surface can be removed in large pieces and discarded.

Chicken Soup with Egg-and-Cheese Flakes

Stracciatella   *To serve 4 to 6*

2 eggs
2 tablespoons freshly grated imported Parmesan cheese
2 teaspoons finely chopped fresh parsley, preferably the flat-leaf Italian type
A few gratings of nutmeg or a pinch of ground nutmeg
Pinch of salt
1 quart chicken stock, fresh or canned

1. In a small bowl, beat the eggs until they are just blended; then mix in the cheese, parsley, nutmeg and salt.
2. Bring the chicken stock to a bubbling boil in a heavy 2- to 3-quart saucepan over high heat.
3. Pour in the egg mixture, stirring gently and constantly with a whisk, and simmer, still stirring, for 2 or 3 minutes.
4. The egg-and-cheese mixture will form tiny flakes in the stock.
5. Taste for seasoning, then ladle the soup into a tureen or individual soup bowls and serve it at once.

Chicken Soup with Egg Drops

To serve 8

A 5-pound chicken
3 quarts boiling water
1 tablespoon salt
2 carrots, sliced
1 onion
2 celery stalks with their leaves
1 parsnip
3 sprigs parsley
2 sprigs dill
1 egg
⅛ teaspoon salt
3 tablespoons flour
3 tablespoons cold water
1 tablespoon minced parsley

1. Wash the chicken and its giblets and put them into the boiling water.
2. Add the tablespoon of salt, cover, and cook over low heat for 1 hour.
3. Add the carrots, onion, celery, parsnip, parsley sprigs and dill, cover again, and cook for 1½ hours.
4. Strain the soup into a clean pan and taste for seasoning.
5. Beat the egg yolk with a fork, then blend in the salt, flour, cold water and minced parsley.
6. Bring to a boil again and, with the tip of a teaspoon, drop the egg mixture bit by bit into the soup.
7. When all the batter has been added, cover the pan tightly and cook over low heat for 10 minutes.

A ceramic hen and chick hover solicitously over a bowl of *canja*, a Portuguese chicken soup that is served with garnishes of lemon and fresh mint.

Chicken Soup with Lemon and Mint

Canja To serve 6

A 3½- to 4-pound stewing fowl, securely trussed
The fowl's giblets — heart, gizzard and liver — finely chopped
2 quarts water
1 cup finely chopped onions
1½ teaspoons salt
3 tablespoons raw medium- or long-grain regular-milled rice, or imported short-grain rice
¼ cup fresh lemon juice
6 tablespoons finely cut fresh mint

1. Place the chicken and its giblets in a heavy 3- to 4-quart casserole.
2. Pour in the water and bring to a boil over high heat, meanwhile skimming off the foam and scum as they rise to the surface.
3. Add the onions and salt and reduce the heat to low.
4. Simmer partially covered for 2½ hours, then add the rice and simmer for 30 minutes or until the chicken and rice are tender.
5. Remove the casserole from the heat and transfer the chicken to a plate.
6. When the bird is cool enough to handle, remove the skin with a small knife or your fingers. Cut or pull the meat away from the bones. Discard the skin and bones, and cut the meat into strips about ⅛ inch wide and 1 inch long.
7. Just before serving, return the chicken to the casserole, add the lemon juice and taste for seasoning.
8. Bring to a simmer and cook only long enough to heat the chicken through.
9. Place a tablespoon of the cut mint in each of six individual serving bowls, ladle the soup over it and serve at once.

Chicken Ragout Soup

Hühner Ragout Suppe   *To serve 6 to 8*

1 to 1½ pounds chicken parts (necks, wings, backs, giblets)
1 small veal knuckle (about ½ pound)
8 peppercorns
1 teaspoon salt
2½ quarts chicken stock, fresh or canned, or water, or part chicken stock and part water
4 tablespoons butter
½ cup finely chopped onions
½ cup diced carrots (¼-inch chunks)
½ cup diced celery (¼-inch chunks)
½ cup diced parsnips (¼-inch chunks)
2 tablespoons flour
3 tablespoons finely chopped parsley

1. In a 4- or 5-quart casserole or soup kettle, combine the chicken parts, veal knuckle, peppercorns, salt and stock and/or water. Add more stock or water, if necessary, to cover by an inch.

2. Bring the liquid to a boil over high heat, skimming the scum from the surface as it rises.

3. Partially cover the pan and reduce the heat to its lowest point; bubbles should barely break on the surface. Simmer slowly for 1½ to 2 hours.

4. Meanwhile, in a 10- or 12-inch skillet, melt the butter.

5. When the foam subsides, add the onions and cook over moderate heat for 2 to 3 minutes, then add the diced carrots, celery and parsnips. Stir them to coat them with

the butter.

6. Cover the skillet tightly and cook the vegetables over the lowest possible heat for 15 to 20 minutes, or until they are barely tender.

7. Check the pan occasionally and add a tablespoon of the chicken stock from the casserole if necessary to keep the vegetables from browning.

8. Pour the soup through a large sieve into a large bowl.

9. Remove all the edible parts of the chicken and dice them coarsely. Discard the skin, bones, veal knuckle and the peppercorns.

10. Return the stock to the large casserole, skim off as much surface fat as you can, and bring it to a simmer again.

11. Now, off the heat, sprinkle the flour over the vegetables in the skillet.

12. Stir together until the flour is thoroughly absorbed.

13. Still off the heat, gently stir in 2 cups of the simmering stock, then return the skillet to the heat and, stirring constantly, cook for 5 to 10 minutes, or until the stock is smooth and thick.

14. Pour the entire contents of the skillet into the simmering soup stock, whisking all the while.

15. Add the diced chicken and bring the soup almost to a boil, then reduce the heat and simmer, partially covered, for 5 to 10 minutes longer.

16. Taste for seasoning; it may need more salt.

17. Pour the soup into a tureen and add the parsley.

Cockaleekie

To make 4 to 5 quarts soup

A 5½- to 6-pound stewing fowl
5 quarts cold water
10 large leeks, including 2 inches of the green stems, thoroughly washed to remove any hidden pockets of sand, and cut diagonally into ½-inch slices (about 8 cups)
½ cup barley
1 tablespoon salt
2 tablespoons finely chopped parsley

1. Wash the fowl thoroughly inside and out under cold running water.

2. Remove and discard any chunks of fat from the cavity, and place the bird in a 10- to 12-quart soup pot.

3. Pour in the 5 quarts of water and bring to a boil over high heat, meanwhile skimming off the foam and scum that will rise to the surface.

4. Add the leeks, barley and salt, and reduce the heat to low.

5. Partially cover the pot and simmer for 3 to 3½ hours, or until the bird is almost falling apart.

6. Transfer it to a platter and, with a large spoon, skim almost all of the fat from the surface of the soup.

7. When the fowl is cool enough to handle, remove the skin and pull the meat from the bones with your fingers or a small knife.

8. Discard the skin and bones and cut the meat into thin shreds about 2 inches long. Return the meat to the soup.

9. Simmer for 2 or 3 minutes to heat the meat through and then taste the soup for seasoning.

10. To serve, pour the soup into a heated tureen or ladle it into individual soup plates, and sprinkle with chopped parsley.

INDEX

PICTURE CREDITS: The sources for the illustrations which appear in this book are shown below: Cover – Richard Jeffery. 7 – Richard Jeffery. 10 – Fred Lyon from Rapho Guillumette. 13 – Charles Phillips. 15 – Richard Jeffery. 19 – Arie deZanger. 24, 25 – Mark Kauffman. 30 – Michael Rougier. 37, 38, 45, 55 – Milton Greene. 56 – Clayton Price. 61 – Milton Greene. 65 – Brian Seed. 75 – Fred Eng. 76 – Rapho Guillumette.

RECIPE CREDITS: The following books were used as sources for the listed pages: *The Dione Lucas Meat and Poultry Cook Book* by Dione Lucas and Ann Roe Robbins – 8 (1st col.), 32 (2nd col.), 34 (2nd col.), 35, 42 (2nd col.), 53 (1st col). *The Embassy Cookbook* by Allison Williams – 8 (top), 12 (2), 35, 42 (2nd col.), 49 (2), 67, 68 (1st col.), 72 (1st col.), 73 (2nd col.). *Toll House Cook Book* © 1953 by Ruth Wakefield – 58.

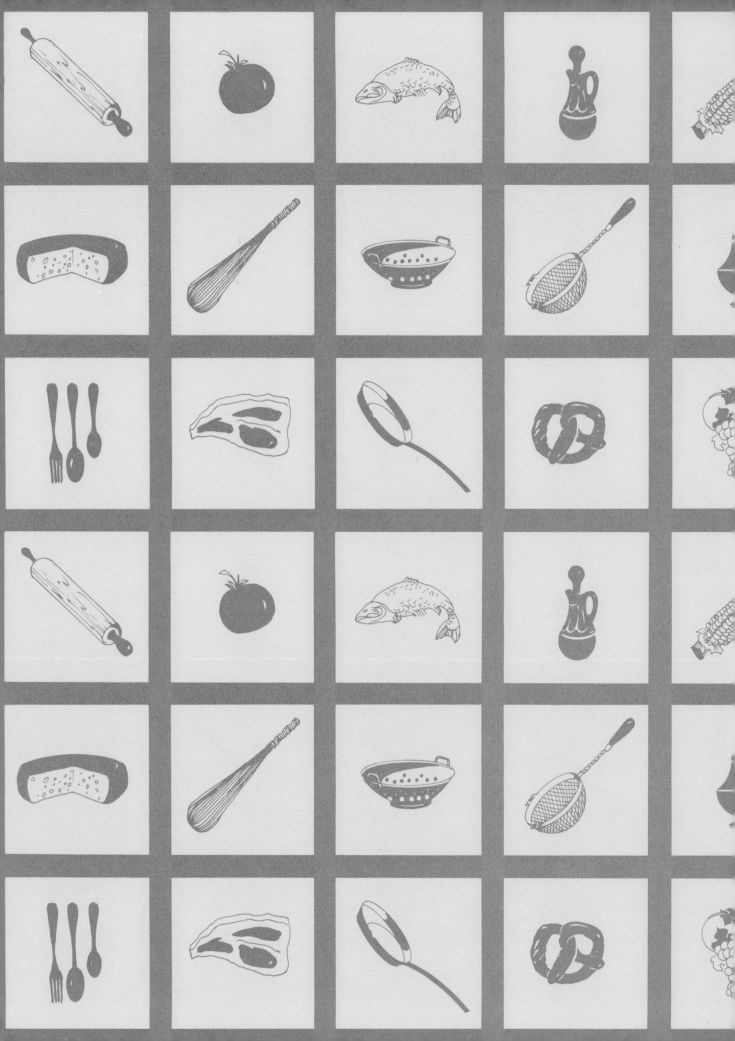